Elementary Science 4

Jeanne Bendick

Roy A. Gallant

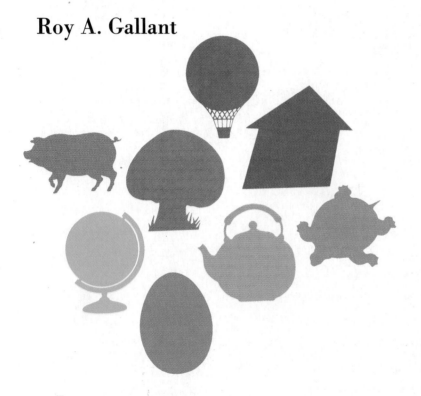

Ginn and Company

DESIGN

Design Office / San Francisco

PRODUCTION

Chestnut House / Norman Baugher

COVER DESIGN

Kirchoff / Wohlberg, Inc.

ILLUSTRATORS

Jerry Beauchamps
Art Ciccone
Kinuko Craft
Chris Leszcynski
Bill Peterson
Yoshi Sekiguchi

PHOTOGRAPHERS

Cover: Tom McHugh / Photo Researchers, Inc.
Lionel Atwell / Peter Arnold: 11 top
R. Backlund / A. Devaney, Inc: 130
James Ballard: 9, 10, 14, 16, 20 top left, 23 right, 31, 39, 45, 46, 50, 51 left, 66, 67, 68, 69, 73, 74, 75, 77, 78, 80, 82, 84, 86, 87, 94, 107, 109 bottom, 126, 127, 134 right, 136, 138, 141 top right, 141 bottom right, 147, 158, 160, 162, 164, 166, 167, 168, 169, 170, 171, 173, 174–175, 178, 179, 180, 181, 184–185, 198–199, 202, 212, 213, 214 inset, 218–219, 220, 221, 223, 225, 228, 230, 233, 234, 235, 236, 237, 238, 239
Dr. H. S. Banton, Jr. / Photo Researchers: 211 right
R. W. Barbour / Photo Researchers: 83, 93
Bill Benoit / Van Cleve: 222
William Berchen / Shostal: 27–28
Don Bishop / Tom Stack & Associates: 29
Rod Borland / Bruce Coleman: 21 top left
G. Mathew Brady / Tom Stack & Associates: 128
Margaret B. Brandon / Tom Stack & Associates: 47
Helen Byram / A. Devaney, Inc: 211 left
Eric Carle / Shostal: 140 top left
Frank Cezus / A. Devaney, Inc.: 112
Bruce Coleman / Bruce Coleman: 190–191
Karen Collidge / Taurus Photos: 134 lower left
Joseph T. Collins / Photo Researchers: 71
Vic Cox / Peter Arnold: 100–101
B. Crader / Tom Stack & Associates: 148–149

Betty Crowell / Van Cleve: 29 inset right
Wm. Curtsinger / Photo Researchers: 129 inset, 139 bottom
Clark Danbar / A. Devaney, Inc: 57, 124–125
Kelly Dean / Photo Researchers: 70
Dr. E. R. Degginger: 12 bottom, 192 top
Nicolas de Vore III / Bruce Coleman: 109 center
Frederick J. Dodd / Peter Arnold: 111
Bob Dusek / A. Devaney, Inc: 110 top
Bob Evans / Peter Arnold: 106 inset
Dan Farber / Photo Researchers: 139 inset
Jack Fields / Photo Researchers: 145
Bob & Miriam Francis / Tom Stack & Associates: 22–23 center
Peter Fronk / Van Cleve: 192 bottom left, 205 bottom
Anthony Galvan III / Taurus Photos: 114
Warren Garst / Tom Stack & Associates: 120 center right
Warren Garst / Van Cleve: 110 inset center left
W. D. Goldberg / A. Devaney, Inc.: 56 top
Mario Grassi / Shostal: 55
Eric Grave / Photo Researchers: 192
Syd Greenberg / Photo Researchers: 209 inset
F. M. Harrison / A. Devaney, Inc.: 143 top
Dr. John F. Hart: 146
Claude Haycraft / Van Cleve: 40
Vance Henry / Taurus Photos: 104 bottom right, 137
D. Herman / A. Devaney, Inc.: 112 left
Jacques Jangoux / Peter Arnold: 108
Yoram Kahana: 95, 203
Yoram Kahana / Peter Arnold: 30
M. P. Kahl / Bruce Coleman: 6–7
Bill Noel Kleeman / Tom Stack & Associates: 65 inset
Barry Klein / A. Devaney, Inc.: 150
William Kopplitz / Tom Stack & Associates: 18, 24, 64, 85, 204
Stephen J. Krasemann / Peter Arnold: 22 bottom right, 32 left
Fred Leavitt / Van Cleve: 29 inset left
Wil Leuchtenberger / Shostal: 12 inset
Harvey Lloyd / Peter Arnold: 15 left
D. C. Lowe / A. Devaney, Inc.: 141 bottom left
John D. Luke / Tom Stack & Associates: 142–143 bottom
Tom McHugh / Photo Researchers: 115 right
Stephen Maka: 72
Tom Meyer / Tom Stack & Associates: 103
Gary Milburn / Tom Stack & Associates: 113 top left

Werner H. Miller / Peter Arnold: 32 center
F. S. Mitchell / Tom Stack & Associates: 116
Michael Moffitt / Taurus Photos: 41 bottom left
R. Morehouse / A. Devaney, Inc.: 227
Dan Morrill: 53, 156–157, 176–177, 229
David Muench / Van Cleve: 62–63
NASA: 51 top right, 56 bottom, 132–133, 140 bottom left, 165
R. Nadillo / A. Devaney, Inc.: 131
John V.A.F. Neal / A. Devaney, Inc.: 38
Nielsen / Peter Arnold: 102 bottom
Bill Peterson: 13 right, 20 inset right, 192 inset top, 193, 195 center right, 195 bottom center, 200
Hans Pfletschinger / Peter Arnold: 25, 90
Dick Pietrcyzk / A. Devaney, Inc.: 104 center
A. J. H. Pullinger / Van Cleve: 195 center left
J. Quigney / A. Devaney, Inc.: 81
Scott Ransom / Taurus Photos: 19 center
L. L. T. Rhodes / A. Devaney, Inc.: 19 bottom right
Edward S. Ross / California Academy of Sciences: 88, 89, 91
H. G. Ross / A. Devaney, Inc.: 113 right, 140 top right
Leonard Lee Rue III / Van Cleve: 73, 104 bottom left, 118
Cindy Rymer / Van Cleve: 214 bottom
Donald Sade / Van Cleve: 65 top
Charles E. Schmidt / Taurus Photos: 119
Len Sherwin / Van Cleve: 13 left
Shostal Assoc. / Shostal: 36–37, 44, 58
Nancy Simmerman / Van Cleve: 129 top
Tom Stack / Tom Stack & Associates: 12, 15 inset right, 106 right, 161
Sumichrast: 11
William Thompson / Shostal: 209 bottom
Darrell Ward / Tom Stack & Associates: 21 top right
Douglas Waugh / Peter Arnold: 102 center left
Bill Weaver / Van Cleve: 17 top
Robert J. Western / Van Cleve: 21 bottom right, 120 center left
William R. Wright / Taurus Photos: 134 upper left
Woods Hole Oceanographic Institution: 152
Yerkes Observatory Photograph: 54
Allen Bruce Zee / Van Cleve: 115 bottom left
Jack Zehart / Shostal: 41 bottom right

Home Office: Lexington, Massachusetts 02173
0–663–36675–5

Preface

Science is an on-going search for truth. Scientists do not say, "Well, that's that. Now I know how it is." Instead, they say, "That is how it seems. Now let's see."

Scientists are not afraid of being wrong. Just like you, they can learn from their mistakes. That is why they keep looking for answers.

Sometimes new questions show that old answers were wrong. That's science!

Jeanne Bendick

Authors

Jeanne Bendick
Roy A. Gallant

Program Director

Dr. J. Myron Atkin

Dean, College of Education
Stanford University
Palo Alto, California

Senior Biological Scientist

Dr. Edward J. Kormondy

Provost and Professor of Biology
University of Southern Maine
Portland, Maine

Senior Physical Scientist

Dr. J. David Gavenda

Professor of Physics and Education
The University of Texas at Austin
Austin, Texas

Contents

Unit 1 Studying Living Things   6

2 Things in the Sky   36

3 Communities   62

4 Mammal Differences   100

5 Our Planet Earth   124

6 Force   156

7 Plant and Animal Cells   190

8 Heat Energy   218

Appendix   245

Glossary   246

Index   251

Unit 1
Studying Living Things

What groups do scientists put things into?

How can you tell what's alive, and what is not?

How many different kinds of living things do you know?

The same or different?

How are a pebble and a beetle the same? Both have rounded shapes. You can find pebbles and beetles on the ground.

How are they different? A beetle has legs and moves. A beetle eats, too.

A beetle moves and eats because it is alive. Living things are active. They do things. Think about yourself. You are a good example of a living thing.

Active living things

Hold your nose for a little while. What happens? You need air. You breathe through your nose or mouth. Living things need air.

Pretend you are playing. A friend throws a ball straight at you. What do you do? You may catch it, or blink your eyes. You might even run away. Living things **react.** They react to movement, heat and cold, and many other things.

react
to act in answer to some action

Look at yourself. Have you always been the same size? All living things grow.

Now think about your parents and your grandparents. They had parents and grandparents, too. All living things can make new living things like themselves. We say that living things **reproduce.**

reproduce
to produce the same kind of living thing

Telling the difference

Now you know four things that living things can do. Can you tell what is alive and what is not? Look at the picture on pages 6 and 7. Can you separate the living things from those that are not alive?

Getting organized

Think of how many different things you have in your room at home. If you wrote down each thing you would have a long list. Sometimes it helps to put things into groups. You could shorten the list if you use groups. You could just write toys, books, and clothes on your list. Would you need other groups?

classify
to divide things that are alike into groups

There are many different kinds of living things on earth. Scientists put them into groups. Putting things that are alike in some way into groups is called **classifying.** Sometimes scientists study unfamiliar things. They compare them to living things they have studied before. Scientists add the "new" living thing to a group that is like it.

Look at the living things on pages 6 and 7. Can you divide them into two groups? Some are plants and some are animals.

Plants and animals

The plants you know best are green. They have roots, stems, and leaves. Many of those plants have flowers. They make seeds, too. All plants need air and water. They do not react as quickly as animals. But they do react.

Animals move more freely than most plants do. Some walk, some swim, some fly. Some don't move at all once they have grown. The way animals move helps to classify them. You will learn more about many kinds of plants and animals.

The in-betweens in water

algae
simple living things that do not have true stems, leaves, or roots

Some living things are more like plants than they are like animals. But they are not true plants. **Algae** (al′jē) are like that. One kind of algae looks like green threads. These algae often grow in ponds. Another kind of algae forms tiny shells. These shells are made of something like glass. You cannot see them without a microscope. Algae grow in fresh water and salt water. Ocean seaweeds are algae.

The in-betweens on land

Fungi (fun′jī) are in-betweens. They live on soil, on logs, and in other places. Mushrooms and toadstools belong to this group. Mushrooms and toadstools grow in many colors. They grow where it is damp. Mushrooms and other fungi grow from spores. Inside a mushroom cap are thousands of **spores.** You can see them clearly.

Molds are fungi, too

You have probably seen molds. Sometimes molds grow on bread or rotting fruit. They look fuzzy. Molds start from spores, too.

fungi
plants that can't
make their own food

spore
reproductive part of
fungi and ferns

mold

mushroom

13

PRINTING WITH A MUSHROOM

You can see the spores from a mushroom. You will need a mushroom, a piece of white paper, a book, and a hand lens.

First, carefully remove the mushroom stem. Place the mushroom cap on the paper, flat side down. Place the book over the mushroom cap. Leave it there for a day. Remove the book and mushroom. The flower shaped print is made of spores. Look at the spores with a hand lens.

What are the little bumps on these fern leaves?

moss

Plants without seeds

Plants without seeds are the oldest kinds of plants on earth. **Moss** is a tiny plant that feels like velvet. Moss doesn't have seeds. The tiny moss plants grow close together. They must grow close together to reproduce. Tiny seedlike things travel from one moss to another.

Ferns are other plants without seeds. Ferns have leaves that look like feathers. In the fall, little bumps form beneath fern leaves. These bumps hold spores. New fern plants grow from the spores. Molds and mushrooms also grow from spores.

corn seed

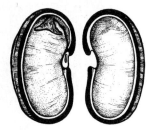

bean seed

Plants with seeds

Seed plants are important to people. Most of the plants you know well grow from seeds. Scientists classify seed plants into groups. Some seeds have only one part. Others have two parts. Peas, beans, apples, and roses are examples of plants with two-part seeds. Lilies, tulips, onions, and corn are examples of plants with one-part seeds.

Flowering plants have seeds. Roses, daisies, and dandelions have seeds. Many wildflowers and weeds grow from seeds. Queen Anne's lace, ragweed, and milkweed grow from seeds.

Some seed plants produce fruits people eat. The fruit we eat

wheat field

is really the container a plant makes for its seeds. The stone inside a cherry is a seed. The pits inside a pumpkin are seeds. What other fruits do you eat? How many can you name?

Grasses have seeds with only one part. There are many kinds of grasses. Some grass seeds are important foods for people and animals. Oats, wheat, rice, and rye are grass seeds.

Trees grow from seeds, too. Trees have many different kinds of seeds. Some of the fruits you like grow on trees. Some trees grow their seeds in **cones.** Redwoods, spruce, and pine trees do that. Think about the trees in your area. What are their names and what kinds of seeds do they have?

cone
a scaly pod with seeds of an evergreen tree

LEARNING ABOUT TREES

You can find out about trees in your neighborhood. Look carefully at their shape. Look at their leaves, seeds, and bark.

Choose a tree to study. You will need paper and pencil, glue, books about trees, and crayons or colored markers.

Draw the whole tree. Show it in fall, winter, spring, and summer if you can.

Draw its leaves, its bark, and its flowers.

Collect fallen seeds or leaves.

Find out its name, places where it grows, and any special information about your tree.

Make a poster with pictures and information.

Many different kinds of living things

Plants and plantlike living things have different shapes and sizes. Think about tiny algae. Then think about giant redwood trees. Remember that they are both plants. Animals can be very different, too. You know all sorts of animals. You know about jellyfish and giraffes, snails and sharks. How do scientists group all the different kinds of animals?

shark

snail

giant redwood

This sponge was once a living thing. On the right, tiny living things can be seen under a microscope.

Almost animals

In the animal world, too, there are in-betweens. Some are not true animals. But they are more like animals than plants. These are tiny "almost animals." They live in pond water. You need a microscope to see them.

Sponges

Sponges are very simple animals. Most of them live in salt water. Their bodies are full of holes. Water and food flow through their bodies. They do not have to move or go hunting. People sometimes use the skeletons of natural sponges for washing.

Animals with bodies like sacs

Water animals with bodies like sacs are another group. These animals have body parts that sting. Some animals in this group have soft bodies. They are the jellyfishes. Other animals in the same group build hard shells. These are corals.

jellyfish

starfish

Other kinds of animals

Sea animals with bumpy skin form another group. They have suction cups for feet. The little cups help them to hold on to things. This starfish is slowly opening a clam shell. Sea urchins and sand dollars also belong to this group. Most animals in this group stay close to one place all their lives.

Animals with soft bodies form another group. Not all of these animals live in water. Garden slugs live on land. So do some snails. They slide along on a slippery foot. Many soft-bodied animals have two shells. Mussels, clams, and scallops have two shells and live in salt water. Some soft-bodied animals have no outer shells at all. The squid and the octopus belong to this group.

Animals with jointed legs

Try to imagine all the animals on earth in one place. Most of them would belong to this next group. These animals have their skeletons on the outside. Each one has many jointed legs. Some crawl along the ocean floors. Some swim. Some walk on land. Still others are at home in the air. Can you think of animals that fit this description? Lobsters, crabs, shrimps, and insects do!

There are more kinds of **insects** than any other kind of animal. There are 250 thousand kinds of beetles. And beetles are only one of 26 major groups of insects. Remember to think of butterflies, dragonflies, ants, bees, wasps, and grasshoppers, too. They are all insects.

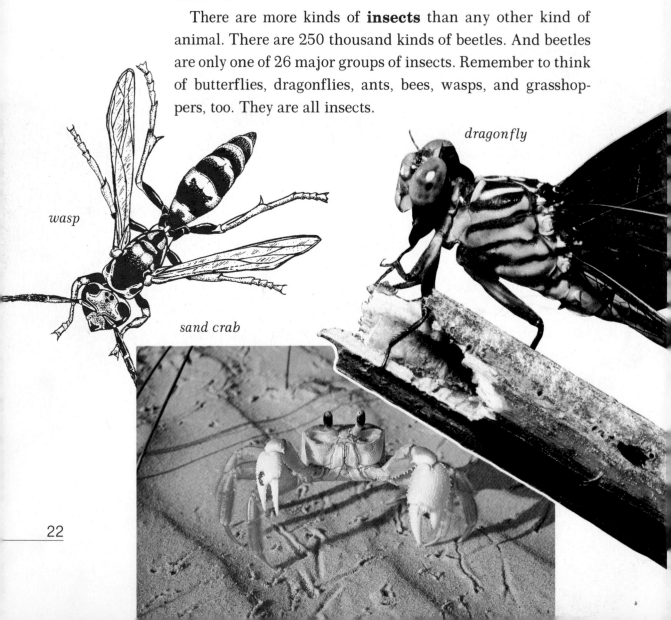

dragonfly

wasp

sand crab

Animals with backbones

Feel the center of your back with your hand. You can feel a line of small bones there. You belong to a large group of animals with **backbones.** Animals with backbones live in water, on land, and in the air.

Fish

Fish have backbones. Fish were on earth long before the dinosaurs were. Fish get the oxygen they need right from the water. Water flows through their mouths. It flows over their **gills** and out of their bodies. Gills take the oxygen out of the water. There are fish of many sizes and shapes. There are tunas and guppies, minnows and sharks.

gill
the breathing organ of an animal that takes oxygen from the water

Amphibians

Some animals with backbones are fun to study. Animals that can live both on land and in water are called **amphibians** (am fib′ē ən). These animals may start out looking like fish but end up with legs. Frogs do that. Amphibians have legs, but they still swim well. Some amphibians can breathe three different ways. They have gills like a fish. They can breathe through their skins. They also have **lungs.** These sacs in their chest fill with air. Amphibians are another kind of "in-between." They are between water animals and land animals.

amphibian
an animal that lives both on land and in water

Reptiles

Long ago, big **reptiles** lived on the earth. They are known as dinosaurs. Some of these reptiles were very big and strong. Tyrannosaurus rex was one of these. The name means "tyrant king." Brontosaurus was a huge reptile. Many kinds of reptiles became **extinct** (eks tingkt′). An animal becomes extinct when all the animals of its kind die.

The reptiles you know best today are snakes, lizards, and turtles.

extinct
no longer found alive anywhere on earth.

26

All reptiles have lungs for breathing. They have backbones, too. Most reptiles reproduce by laying eggs. Reptile eggs have thick shells. Crocodiles and alligators are reptiles. They live in swamps and water. But they return to land to lay their eggs.

alligator

Birds

Some people study birds as a hobby. All birds have feathers, wings, and a beak. Finding differences is the interesting part of bird study.

Birds have backbones. Most of their bones are thin and hollow. Birds are **warm-blooded.** Their bodies can be kept warm even in cold places. Warm-blooded animals can live in more places than **cold-blooded** animals can. Fish, amphibians, and reptiles are all cold-blooded.

Mammals

Mammals are warm-blooded. They have backbones. Nearly all mammals give birth to live young. Mammal babies need care. They drink milk produced in their mothers' bodies. Some mammals have hairy bodies. Others have hair on only some parts of their bodies. Mammals can learn better than other kinds of animals.

One kind of mammal is very special. You will learn a lot about this special mammal. The mammal is you! Human beings are mammals.

The mammal group has many other animals. Bats, cats, bears, and cows are mammals. Kangaroos, whales, anteaters, and giraffes are mammals.

You can find out how many animals and plants you know. Then you can put them in groups.

Get two long pieces of paper. Write **Plants** at the top of one. At the top of the other write **Animals.**

Think about all the plants and animals you know. List their names on the long pieces of paper.

Add new names as you think of them. Paste in pictures you may find of the listed animals and plants.

Now get some sheets of notebook paper. Put the names of groups at the top of each paper. Use the headings from this unit. Read the names from the long pieces of paper. Decide to which of the groups the name belongs. Write the name on that sheet.

Why classify living things?

Can you decide if a plant or an animal belongs in a certain group? Then you know a lot of other things about that plant or animal.

If you see an animal has feathers, you know it's a bird. What else do you know about it? You know it hatched out of an egg, even though you didn't see it happen. You know it has a beak, not teeth. You know these things because of classifying.

Different kinds

A penguin and a woodpecker are both birds. A penguin and a woodpecker are alike in important ways.

But a penguin and a woodpecker are different. They don't look at all alike. They live in different places. They eat different foods. The penguin and the woodpecker are different kinds of birds. No two kinds of animals are exactly alike.

A porpoise, a polar bear, and a person are all mammals. They are alike in important ways. They are different in many ways, too. In what ways are they alike? In what ways are they different? You have to study the animals to know.

SCIENCE ON THE JOB

Game wardens must know a lot about the animals they protect. They study where the animals live. The number and kind of plants and animals are important. They can tell if there is enough food and water. If there is not enough food, the warden can have food brought in. Or animals can be moved to another place.

Game wardens protect the animals under their care, too. They help enforce hunting and fishing laws.

Game wardens work in many areas. Some of these might be beaches, forests, wetlands, or deserts.

REVIEW QUESTIONS

1. What are some of the ways plants are different from animals?
2. What are spores? Name some plants that grow from spores.
3. Name three grass seeds that are good to eat.
4. How do fish breathe?
5. What is the most plentiful kind of animal on earth?
6. How are all birds alike?
7. Name four things all living things do.
8. Tell what you know about reptiles.
9. Why are classifications useful?

WORDS TO REVIEW

algae	extinct	react
amphibian	fungi	reproduce
backbone	gill	reptile
classify	insect	sponge
cold-blooded	lung	spore
cone	mammal	warm-blooded

EXPLORING FURTHER

1. Find out more about a group of plants or animals. Find pictures. Find information. Use an encyclopedia or some library books. Write a report about a group of living things.

2. Spend an hour looking for animals near your school. See what animals live in the soil, in the trees, and in other places. Look for signs of animals. Look for fur, feathers, footprints, and droppings. Find out about the animals around you.

3. Make a list of animals that are extinct. Collect drawings and models of these animals. Find out why these animals became extinct. Are other animals alive today in danger of becoming extinct?

4. Here are some books about living things. You may wish to read some of them.

   STRANGE DIFFERENCES by D. X. Fenten

   THE HIDDEN WORLD: LIFE UNDER A ROCK by Laurence Pringle

   NATURE IN THE CITY: PLANTS by Joan Elma Rahn

   ANIMALS IN YOUR NEIGHBORHOOD by Seymour Simon

Unit 2
Things in the Sky

Is the moon bigger than the stars?

What is a rainbow?

What are flying saucers?

Why is the sky blue?

Look out at the sky right now. It may not be blue. It may be covered with white **clouds.** It may be gray with rain clouds. At night the sky is black with lots of **stars.**

On a clear day, the sky is blue. The gas that we call air makes it look blue. There is dust in the air. There are tiny drops of water, too. These things scatter the sun's light in all directions. The scattered light is so bright that it hides the stars in the daytime. Without the air, the sky would look black. Then we could see stars even in the daytime.

SCATTERING LIGHT

Put a small amount of dust or sand into a jar. Shake the jar. Hold the jar in the sunlight. What happens to the light? If there is no bright sunlight, use a flashlight or hold the jar up to the room lights. The more dust there is, the more the light is scattered.

Sunlight

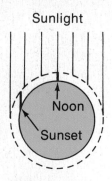

Sunlight

Noon

Sunset

horizon
the line where the
sky and the earth
seem to meet

The sun is the brightest object in the sky. The sun's light is very strong. You should never look straight at the sun. The strong light could damage your eyes.

There is a time when it is safe to look at the sun. That time is at sunset. Sunset happens because the earth is always turning. When it turns away from the sun, it will be night. Just before night, we have to look near the **horizon** for the sun. This means that the sun's light has to go through a lot of air.

Look at the diagram. You can measure how far the sun's light has to travel through air. If the sun's light travels through more air, it will meet more dust and water drops. Can you tell why the sunlight is not as strong at sunset?

40

The moon

After the sun, the moon is the brightest thing in the sky. The moon does not make its own light. It **reflects** light from the sun. Sunlight strikes the moon. Some of the sun's light is bounced back to earth.

You can look at the moon. The sun's light reflected from the moon is not strong enough to hurt your eyes.

The moon can sometimes be seen during the day. Look at the sky on your way to school. You might see the moon.

When the moon is near the horizon, it looks orange. It also looks much bigger. Can you tell why this is so?

Notice how much larger the moon looks near the horizon (on right) than higher in the sky.

When sunlight passed through more air, it was safe to look at. Particles in the air scattered much of the light in other directions. The same thing happens to sunlight when it bounces off the moon. Look at the diagram on page 40. The moon looks orange or dark yellow when it is near the horizon. It also looks bigger.

Keeping records

People have always looked at the sky. They kept records of things that happened. Then they could see if these things happened again. They could see if things happened the same way.

Here are some records. What can you tell about sunrise in October? What can you tell about sunset?

October		
Day	Sunrise	Sunset
1	6:35	6:25
2	6:36	6:22
3	6:38	6:21
4	6:39	6:19
5	6:41	6:18
6	6:43	6:17
7	6:44	6:15

NOW YOU WILL KEEP SOME RECORDS

Keep a record of the way the moon looks. Make a chart like this one. Use pictures to show what the moon looked like. Put in the date. Put in morning or evening.

Keep the record for one month. You may see other things, too. Write down what you observe.

You can see the moon's shape change day by day. Sometimes you will not be able to see the moon. Leave the space blank for that day.

Your teacher will draw a big circle on the chalkboard in front of your room. Hold a penny or small cardboard circle out in front of you. Close one eye. The penny should look like it is inside the circle. Now slowly move the penny closer to your eye. What happens to the circle on the chalkboard?

Things don't always look the same. It depends on how you look at them. The more ways you can look at something, the more you can find out about it.

The circle at the front of the room is like the sun. The penny is like the moon. The sun is much, much bigger than the moon. But in the sky they look like they are the same size. Now can you tell why?

When you are in a car, the car looks big. Other cars far down the road look small, like toys. Are they really as small as toy cars? When you look up at an airplane, it looks small. It could be carrying 200 people. Is it really small?

Many thousands of years ago, when people first started to notice the world around them, they thought that everything was the way it seemed to be. Earth seemed flat under their feet. They believed that earth was flat.

They said earth was bigger than the sun and the moon and the stars. It seemed to be.

At night, when they looked up at the sky, the stars seemed to be all around them. So they said that earth was in the center of all the stars.

They said earth never moved. They couldn't see it move or feel it move or hear it move. Is that the way things seem to you?

People made up stories to explain what they saw. They said that the sun was a god who drove a chariot across the sky every day. They said that the moon was the queen of night.

They made up stories about earth and the seasons.

Some people looked harder. They noticed more things. They kept records and asked a lot of questions.

They asked:

Why do things happen the way they do?

What if things are not the way they seem to be?

Are there other ways to look at them?

Are there other ways to think about them?

Changing ideas

Most people don't like to change old ideas. Do you?

Suppose the things you see seem to tell you that you are living on a flat earth that does not move.

Then suppose someone says to you, "What if earth is not flat? I think earth is a round ball. And I think it moves. It turns and it moves through space." Would you believe the person? Would you want to believe the person?

It is not easy when you first begin to think about living on a round ball that is whirling through space. Maybe you think you would get dizzy. Maybe you think you would fall off.

It is easier to think that you are living on something that is big and flat and does not move. It is easy to believe that earth is the biggest thing there is. When you look around, that is the way it seems to be.

It is hard to believe that earth is just a speck in space. The sun is just a speck, too, but it is more than a million times bigger than earth. Can you even imagine "a million times bigger"?

We know that those hard-to-believe ideas are true. But it took a long, long time to be sure. It took a lot of looking. It took a lot of record-keeping. It took a lot of model-building.

What is a model for?

Do you have a model car? Does it look like a real car? How is it different from a real car? The people who make real cars make model cars first to show how the real car will look. That is one reason for making a **model.**

Sometimes we make a model to see how something works. A paper airplane is a kind of model. You can learn a lot about flying from paper airplanes.

Sometimes we build models of things that are hard to see. Maybe they are too small. Maybe they are too big. Maybe we don't even know how something looks at all. How can you make a model of something you have never seen?

You start by using everything you do know about it. Then try out ideas to see if they work with your model. A globe is a model of earth. We have used that model for hundreds of years.

Before people went out into space, nobody had ever seen the whole, round earth. But when we finally got to see earth from space, it looked like the model.

What is it?

Have you seen other things while keeping your moon records? Beneath a rain cloud, many drops of water are in the air. When light passes through water, it bends. Some colors bend more than others. Light from the sun contains all different colors. These are called the colors of the **spectrum.** The chart shows the colors. When sunlight goes through raindrops the colors are spread out to make a **rainbow.** A picture of a rainbow is on page 36. Can you find the colors of the spectrum in the rainbow?

spectrum
the band of colors produced when light is broken up

rainbow
a curve of colors across the sky

Clouds

You have seen many types of clouds—big and fluffy, thin and wispy. Sometimes the clouds cover the whole sky. If you have been in an airplane, you may have flown through clouds. **Fog** is a low cloud.

Clouds and fog are made of the same thing. Tiny drops of water hang in the air. The drops form when warm, humid air is cooled.

Another kind of cloud is made by airplanes. These clouds are called **contrails.** They look like long thin lines in the sky. Air coming off the wing tips of an airplane is cooled slightly. Water drops form in the cooler air.

The night sky

On a clear night you can see stars. You might see the moon or planets. But you may also see some strange things. A streak of light may move across the sky. If it were cloudy, you would think it was lightning. But on a clear night, that was probably a **meteor.** The flash of light was really a fast-moving piece of space rock. When the rock bumped into the air around the earth, it got hot. It got so hot that it glowed brightly. It burned up! Other times, the rock is not all burned. Chunks of the rock can land on the earth.

meteor
piece of space material that burns up before reaching earth

Northern lights

Dancing lights can appear over the North Pole. The lights can be of many colors. Long fingers of light stretch out across the sky. The lights are very beautiful.

Aircraft

Other objects in the sky are made by people. Some of these things are call **aircraft.** Airplanes, gliders, and balloons are aircraft. Airplanes look different at night. Red, green, and white lights are used to mark the airplanes. From far away the airplane may look like a star.

aircraft
object that can be floated or flown through the air

Spacecraft

Space satellites circle the earth. They were sent into space on rockets. At night they can reflect the sunlight. If you see a tiny light moving across the sky, it may be a **spacecraft.**

spacecraft
vehicle used for travel outside the earth's air layer

Weather balloons

Wind speed and air temperature are measured by weather balloons. These balloons do not have lights. But a balloon can reflect light from the earth or the sun. A balloon flying low can look like a strange moon.

Can you think of other things that can be seen in the sky?

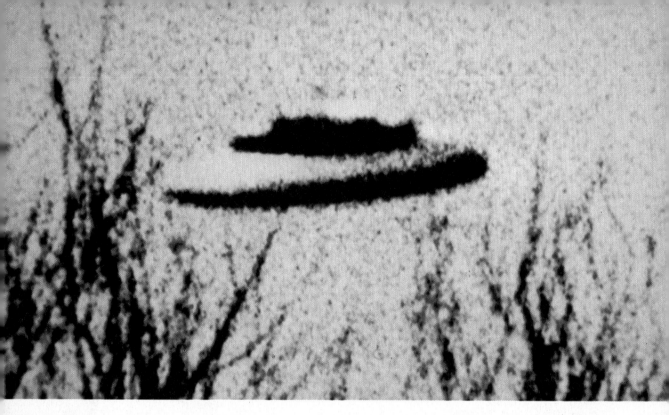

What could this be?

"UFOs"

UFO
unknown object in
the sky

Strange things in the sky are sometimes called flying saucers.
They can also be called **"UFOs."**

The letters UFO stand for Unidentified Flying Object. It
means that you don't know what an object up in the sky is.
Anything you see in the sky can be a UFO. Some people think
UFOs are spaceships from a strange place. But a UFO can be
an airplane. It can be a weather balloon or a satellite. It can be
anything that you can't name.

It is dark at night. But there is always a little light. And that
light can play tricks on your eyes. You have seen some of these
"tricks" in this unit. Now when you look at the sky you will
know more about what you see.

58

SCIENCE ON THE JOB

You have seen busy streets with a lot of automobile traffic. Traffic lights, signs, and police officers help to control this traffic.

There is also a lot of traffic in the sky! At some airports, airplanes are landing or taking off every 30 seconds. People who help these airplanes come and go safely are called air traffic controllers.

Air traffic controllers must know the location of each airplane near an airport. They must watch the sky every minute. This is done by observing radar screens. They talk to pilots by radio and guide them to safe landings and take-offs.

This is an exciting job for a person who can see well and think fast. Knowing about things in the sky helps, too.

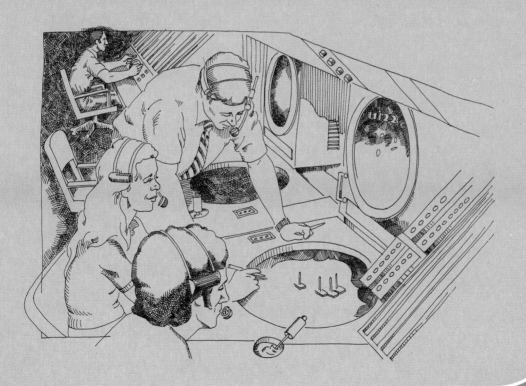

REVIEW QUESTIONS

1. What time of the day is sunlight the weakest? Draw a picture to show why it is not as strong at this time of the day.

2. Name the second brightest object in the sky. How does it get its light?

3. The later the sun sets, the longer the day lasts. What months of the year does the sun shine longest where you live?

4. If the night is clear you can see the most stars from a place where there are no bright lights. Name some good places for star watching.

5. Name some planets that you can see in the night sky.

6. The sun is much bigger than the moon. Why do they look about the same size in the sky?

7. Look at an airplane in the sky. Do you think it is moving faster or slower than it looks? Explain your answer.

8. By asking good questions, people learned more about earth in space. Name some things you have learned by asking good questions.

9. A map of the world and a globe are both models of the earth. Which do you think is a better model? Why?

10. Wouldn't it be fun to walk through a cloud? You can walk through something just like a cloud without leaving earth. How can you do this?

11. Sometimes people look in the sky and see lights they cannot identify. What are some of the things they could have seen?

WORDS TO REVIEW

aircraft	meteor	rainbow	spectrum
contrail	model	reflect	star
horizon	planet	spacecraft	UFO

EXPLORING FURTHER

1. Some people think that we shouldn't say, "The sun rises in the morning and sets at night," because that is not the way it is. How do you feel about that? Could you think of a better way to tell what happens?

2. How do you feel about changing old ideas for new ones? Do you think it's hard? What do you think might happen if there were a law against changing ideas?

3. You may have heard some tales about the moon. Have you heard the tale about the "man in the moon", or "the moon is made of green cheese"? When you look at the moon, can you imagine a man living there? Is the moon really made of cheese? Why do you think people made up stories like this?

4. Have a contest to see who can build the best model airplane. Make the airplane models out of sheets of paper. The "best" model is the one that travels the longest distance. Do all the airplanes fly well? Why do you think airplane engineers make a model of their ideas before building the real plane?

5. Here are some books you might like to read. They are about some of the things you learned in this unit.

   UFO by Rhoda Blumberg

   LET'S GO ON A SPACE SHUTTLE by Michael Chester

   THE TRUE BOOK OF SPINOFFS FROM SPACE by Leila Boyle Gemme

   COLONIES IN ORBIT: THE COMING AGE OF HUMAN SETTLEMENTS IN SPACE by David C. Knight

   CHARLIE BROWN'S SECOND SUPER BOOK OF QUESTIONS AND ANSWERS by Charles M. Schultz

Unit 3
Communities

Could you teach an ant to do tricks?

What will make a frog jump?

Can you build a community?

Your community

Where do you live? Do you live in a city? Do you live in a small town? Where you live is called a **neighborhood.**

A neighborhood is a place made up of living and nonliving things. Your neighborhood is made up of houses, trees, grass, cats, and many other things. What other things are in your neighborhood?

All the living things in your neighborhood make up your **community.** The trees, grass, and cats are part of your community. What else is in your community?

neighborhood
a place made up of living and nonliving things

community
all the plants and animals that live together in the same place

Communities in nature

Plants and animals live in special places. Some plants and animals live best where it is hot and damp. This monkey is part of a jungle community.

Other things live best where it is hot and dry. This lizard is part of a desert community.

A pond contains a community. A forest has another kind of community. A rain puddle can have a community, too.

Could you make a community? You could make one in a glass container. A glass container in which you keep living things is called a **terrarium** (tə rãr′ē əm).

Go to a place where you can find plants and animals. A woods would be a good place. It has plants and animals and soil.

You will be collecting things. So take plastic containers and bags. Take spoons to dig with.

Scoop up some soil. Does it feel soft and damp? Are there some twigs in the soil? Put some of the soil and twigs into a plastic container. Collect green plants and seeds, too.

Take a stone with some moss growing on it. Put it in a plastic bag.

Take these things back to the classroom. Now you are ready to build your terrarium.

BUILDING A TERRARIUM

Put pebbles and sand into a big glass container. Pebbles and sand make spaces where air and water can go. Put your collected soil on top of the sand. Add the rock and some twigs. Put in ferns and other plants.

A small dish of water in one corner of the terrarium can be a pond.

Sprinkle the plants and soil with water.

Where should you keep your terrarium? Bright sunlight will make your terrarium too warm. So keep your terrarium in a shady place. Then, the plants will grow well.

ADDING ANIMALS

What kinds of animals would you add to this terrarium? What animals live in the damp woods?

Frogs and turtles live by ponds. Under a leaf or rock in the woods you may see a salamander. You might even find a chameleon (kə mē′lē ən). These are some animals you may find in a woodland.

Collect some of these animals for your terrarium. Perhaps you can find other kinds of animals for your terrarium.

Have you ever moved into a new town? Maybe you have gone to a new school. Did it take a while for you to feel at home?

The terrarium is a new place for the animals to live. Will the animals have the same problem?

Salamanders have smooth skin.

One chameleon will have a mark.

Animals that look alike

You may have put two animals of the same kind in your terrarium. They may look alike. How can you tell them apart? Two animals may look so much alike that you can't tell which is which.

Make a spot on one with a bright-colored, waterproof marker. Then you will be able to tell them apart.

A place of its own

When you put animals into the terrarium, don't crowd them. A few animals can live there very well for a long time. If you have too many animals, they will fight. Animals fight each other for food or a place to stay.

Many animals defend the spaces they need for living. An animal's living space is called its **territory.** Sometimes they will defend just a small territory—their nest. Sometimes they will defend a larger territory—the place where they look for food.

territory
an animal's living space

Toads feed on insects.

Perhaps you put a frog in your terrarium. At first the frog will hop around the terrarium. Then it will "stake out a claim" to one special place. It will spend most of its time there. When you look for the frog, you'll know just where to look.

Once the frog is settled in its territory, add another frog. Or, you might add a toad.

What do you think will happen if the new frog or toad is much bigger or smaller than the other one? If there is plenty of room in the terrarium, then maybe the big one won't bother the little one. But if they are crowded for space, watch what happens.

If you are going to have only frogs and toads, you won't have room for many, because each one will need a territory.

Cricket frog

A shell covers most of a turtle's body.

Room for one more?

Is there room for a salamander (sal′ə man′dər) in the terrarium? Salamanders live in damp, woodsy places. You would find them under rotting leaves and bark. One or two salamanders could live under the rocks and leaves in the terrarium.

Is there a place for another animal to live? What about one that lives mostly in water? A small turtle could live in the pond dish. It won't bother the frogs. The frogs won't bother it. The turtle may spend part of the time on land. But it can live peacefully with the frogs and the salamanders.

Have you used up all the living space in the terrarium?

Not all woodland animals live on the ground. Some woodland animals live in the trees. The larger plants in your terrarium are like trees. Could some animals live in those "trees"?

Tree frogs are very small—about the size of your thumb. Do you think they could live with the other animals? Try it and see. Put a tree frog in your terrarium.

Does the tree frog live in the territory of the bigger frogs? Where does it spend most of its time?

Spring peeper

More animals

Other animals live in the trees, too. What tree animals do you know? The American chameleon lives in a tree.

Could you put two chameleons in your terrarium? Two could live there if one is a male and the other is a female. Two females could live there, too. But both should be about the same size. If one is much larger than the other, the larger one will chase the smaller one. It might even eat it.

If both chameleons are males, they will probably fight. You can tell a male chameleon by an extra-loose flap of pink skin under his throat. This is a **dewlap.**

Animals live in the woodland soil, too. What animals can you name that live in the soil?

Earthworms live in the soil. Sow bugs are soil animals, too. Put some soil animals in your terrarium.

Chameleon

Earthworm

74

Living space

You have salamanders under the rocks and leaves.

You have a turtle in the pond.

You have frogs, toads, or both, each in its own territory.

You have chameleons, and maybe a tree frog.

You have soil animals, too.

These animals will use up all the living space in the terrarium.

WATCHING ANIMAL BEHAVIOR

How an animal acts is called its **behavior.** You can watch an animal's behavior. Watch the animals in your terrarium. Write down things that the animals do.

Keep a record book. Make a place to write each of these things: the kind of animal you are watching, the date, the time of day, what you did, and how the animal behaved. Your record could look like this:

Kind of Animal	Date	Time of Day	What I Did	How the Animal Behaved

What makes an animal behave?

Were you ever frightened by a loud noise? Did you jump?

The loud noise was a **stimulus** (stim′yə ləs). A stimulus is something that makes an animal behave. The smell of food can be a stimulus. How does the smell of food make you behave?

How you behave is called a **response** (ri spons′). If you jump when you hear a loud noise, that is your response. You responded to the stimulus of noise. The loud noise made you behave.

stimulus
a change inside or around a living thing that makes it respond

response
the reaction of a living thing to a stimulus

You can find out about animal behavior.

Look carefully. Is the animal changing its color? Is the animal changing its position?

Listen. Is the animal making a noise?

How is the animal behaving? What is the stimulus? What is the animal's response? Why is the animal behaving this way?

Sometimes you can see the stimulus and the response. If you put a live fly into the terrarium, the frog will jump to catch it. It's easy to see the stimulus (fly) and response (frog jumps). But sometimes it's not so easy.

Sometimes you can see the stimulus, but not the response. If you put a hot, bright light near a turtle, the heat makes the turtle's temperature go up. The light is a stimulus. It is easy to see. But you can't see the turtle's temperature change. You cannot see that response. But you might see the turtle move away if it gets too hot. That is a response, too.

Sometimes you can see the response but not the stimulus. If a chameleon suddenly puffs up its dewlap, that's a response you can easily see. But what caused this change in the chameleon's behavior? You cannot see the stimulus. It could be something inside the chameleon.

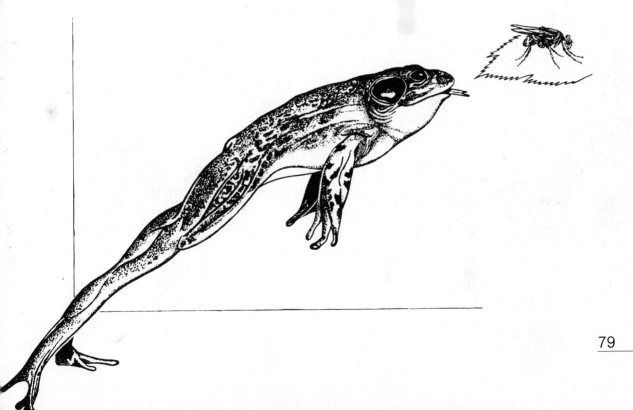

Chameleons

Chameleons are **reptiles.** Reptiles have scaly skin. Look closely at a chameleon. Look at its skin with a hand lens. You can see the scales that make up the chameleon's skin.

Give the chameleons insects and earthworms. Do they eat them? Can you teach chameleons to eat out of your hand? Remember to record what you try. Record the stimulus. Record how the chameleons respond.

Do your chameleons drink water? Do you ever see them near the terrarium pond? Put the chameleons right next to the pond. Do they drink the water? Put them in the pond. Do they swim? Sprinkle water on some leaves with a sprayer. Do they drink any of this?

What other ways can you think of to find out how chameleons behave?

Turtles

Turtles are fun to watch. They live in shells made of bone. Turtles are reptiles, too.

What things can you find out about the behavior of a turtle? Where does a turtle sit when part of the terrarium is in the sun? Feed insects to the turtle. Where does it eat them? Many turtles must eat underwater. Is your turtle like that? How can you find out?

Frogs

Frogs are **amphibians** (am fib′ē ən). The word amphibian means two lives. These animals live part of their lives in water. They live part of their lives on land.

A frog's skin is smooth and moist. The front legs are shorter than the back legs. Frogs eat worms and insects. They catch live insects with their tongues.

Watch the frog in your terrarium. Can you find out other things about a frog? Be sure to write down what you see.

Here are some things you may want to find out. How do frogs protect themselves? Do they hide? Do they jump away? Do they puff up? Do frogs make noises? What kinds of noises do frogs make? When do frogs make noises?

Toads

Toads are amphibians, too. Toads have bumps on their bodies. These bumps contain a bad-tasting liquid. Most animals do not like the taste of this liquid. So they leave the toads alone.

Does your toad like to drink water? What does your toad like to eat? What do you think is the most interesting thing about the behavior of your toad?

Salamanders

Salamanders are amphibians, like frogs and toads. Salamanders live under leaves and moss. They live in dead tree stumps, too. Sometimes you will find a salamander under the bark of a tree. Salamanders eat worms and insects.

How can you find out about the ways a salamander behaves? Can you get a salamander to eat chopped meat? If you shine a light on a salamander, what will it do?

Ants

Ants live in a woodland, too. Ants are social **insects.** Social insects behave as part of a group. One ant doesn't live by itself. One ant does not get food for itself the way one frog or one turtle does. Ants live and work together.

Wherever you live, you can find ants to watch. You can find them in the yard or the park or in a vacant lot. If you follow the ants, you can find their nests. Ants always go back to their nests.

insect
a small, air-breathing animal without a backbone, but with a three-part body and three pairs of legs

MAKING AN ANT HOME

You can make an ant home. First, find an ant nest out-of-doors. Scoop it up with a shovel. Pick up all the ants you can find. Take some of the dirt or sand from the ant hill. Put these all together in a jar. If you are lucky, you will find eggs or **larvae** (lär'vē) in the nest, too—maybe a whole pile of them.

Look for the queen ant. She is much bigger than the others. Every nest has a queen. Put the queen in the jar, too. Take all your ants from one nest. If you mix two nests, the ants will fight. That's how ants behave.

Put a piece of damp sponge in the jar. Cover the jar tightly with nylon stocking. Stand the jar in a pan of water. This will keep any ants from escaping into the classroom.

Put some food in the jar. Add a few drops of sugar water, a few cookie crumbs, and a tiny bit of fruit. Feed the ants just a little every day.

Keep the soil or sand in the jar slightly damp. Watch the ants build their rooms and tunnels.

When you are not watching the ants, keep the jar covered with a cardboard box. An ant nest in the soil is always dark.

Keep a record of what you observe.

Instinct

Ants are born knowing how to do the things they do. This kind of build-in behavior is called **instinct** (in'stingkt). Instincts make ants behave the way they do.

Other animals behave only by instinct, too. A caterpillar doesn't plan to spin itself into a cocoon. A spider doesn't choose the shape of its web. Bees don't pick a queen bee. These animals don't make choices.

All animals have some instincts. Instincts help to keep animals alive and going.

Baby chicks run if they see the shadow of a hawk. Baby kittens hiss when they first see a dog.

When you were a baby, nobody had to teach you how to suck or swallow. Nobody had to teach you how to hold onto things. These are instincts you were born with.

instinct
unlearned behavior that an animal is born with

92

Some animals can learn

Birds learn as soon as they begin to hatch. They learn even before they are out of the egg. This becomes part of the way birds behave. No matter what happens later, they cannot unlearn it.

A baby duck will become attached to the first moving thing it sees. That thing might be the mother duck. But it might also be a wind-up toy. It might be a person. This kind of learning is called **imprinting.**

imprinting
behavior learned early in life that involves recognizing and being attracted to something

Other ways to learn

Some animals learn in still another way. Some animals have a memory. They learn by **experience.**

A rat, for example, can learn by experience. It can learn to run through many paths to find food. If some paths are blocked and new ones are opened, the rat can learn the new paths.

Even the most intelligent animals have instincts. They can also learn by experience. But some can do other things, too. They can **reason.** They can figure things out. They can decide what to do. Some animals can solve a problem in their mind, without acting it out first.

What animals can you think of that behave like that?

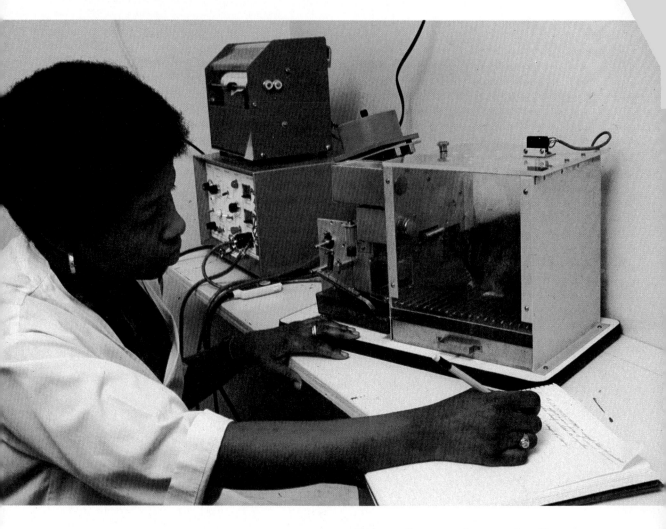

Lab worker records an animal's response to a stimulus.

Many ways to behave

Animals behave in many ways. They behave by instinct, as an ant does. They behave by instinct and imprinting, as a duck does. They behave by instinct and experience, as a rat does.

How do you behave? You behave by instinct, experience, and reasoning.

95

SCIENCE ON THE JOB

Have you ever trained a pet to do a trick? When you train something, you teach it. Police dogs are taught to do police jobs. Many other kinds of animals are taught to do jobs, too. Some of these are dolphins, police horses, and seeing-eye dogs.

Teaching people is easier. Humans are the smartest animals on earth. Your parents are teachers. They taught you things before you went to school. If you have ever taught someone something, you are a teacher, too.

School teachers have learned special ways of teaching. They know what to teach. And they know how to help you learn. Are you an easy person to teach?

97

REVIEW QUESTIONS

1. What is a community?
2. In your terrarium, what did you have to provide for the living things?
3. Name three animals that live in a woodland.
4. What is behavior?
5. What is a territory?
6. Name some reptiles. Name some amphibians.
7. What might happen if a community becomes too crowded?

WORDS TO REVIEW

amphibian	insect	response
behavior	instinct	stimulus
community	larva	terrarium
dewlap	neighborhood	territory
imprinting	reptile	

EXPLORING FURTHER

1. No two animals in a terrarium behave in the same way. The behavior of every frog is just a little bit different from that of every other frog. Sometimes you can tell one frog from another by the way it acts. Watch the responses of two similar frogs. What differences in behavior do you notice?

2. What happens when you put a large jar in the place where your frog usually sits? Does the frog sit next to it? Does the frog choose another favorite spot? Does it try to move the jar away?

3. Do big animals always push smaller animals around? Watch the animals in your terrarium. Watch animals outside. Have you ever seen a little bird attacking a large crow? Does a little dog sometimes scare off a bigger dog?

4. Look at some skin that was shed by the chameleon. Can you see through it? Look at it with a hand lens. What do you see?

5. Here are some books you might like to read. They are about some of the things you learned in this unit.

    A PLACE TO LIVE by Jeanne Bendick

    HOW ANIMALS BEHAVE by Jeanne Bendick

    I WATCH FLIES by Gladys Conklin

    THE BIRD'S WOODLAND: WHAT LIVES THERE by Richard Farrar

    WOODLANDS AROUND THE WORLD by Corinne Naden

    TERRARIUMS by Alice Parker

    A CLOSER LOOK AT ANTS by Valerie Pitt and David Cook

Mammal Differences

Do whales have hair?

What do your bones do for you?

Can horses walk on their toes?

Many kinds of mammals

Elephants and people, whales and bats, cows and cats, and kangaroos all look different. Some are big, and some are small. They may be many different colors. But they are all mammals.

They live in different places, and they eat different things. They move in different ways. But mammals are alike in some important ways. What do you think some of those ways are?

Koala bears and porcupine, top. Rhinoceros, bottom.

Mammals have live young

All animals **reproduce** themselves. They make other animals of the same kind. Most animals start as eggs.

reproduce
to produce the same kind of living thing

Some animals lay eggs. The young animals hatch from these eggs. Birds lay eggs. Many fish lay eggs. So do frogs and some snakes.

But other animals grow and change inside their mother before they are born. Mammals are like that. Most mammals give birth to live young.

Mammals produce milk

Mammals grow and develop inside their mother before they are born. Mammals need more care after they are born than the young of other kinds of animals. They cannot find food for themselves. They need to be taken care of.

A mammal mother makes milk inside her body to feed her young. Other kinds of animals can't do that. Milk is the first food young mammals eat.

Mammals have hair

All mammals have hair on their bodies. Some mammals have wooly hair all over their bodies. A sheep is covered with wooly hair. What can a sheep's wooly hair be used for?

Some mammals have stiff hair. A pig's hair is stiff. It can be used in paintbrushes and hairbrushes.

Some mammals have smooth, flat hair. Horses do, and so do tigers.

Some mammals, like rabbits and beavers, have soft hair. We call it fur, but it is hair.

Other mammals have hair on only some parts of their bodies. People have hair like that.

Some mammals have hardly any hair at all. Whales have just a few whiskers around the mouth.

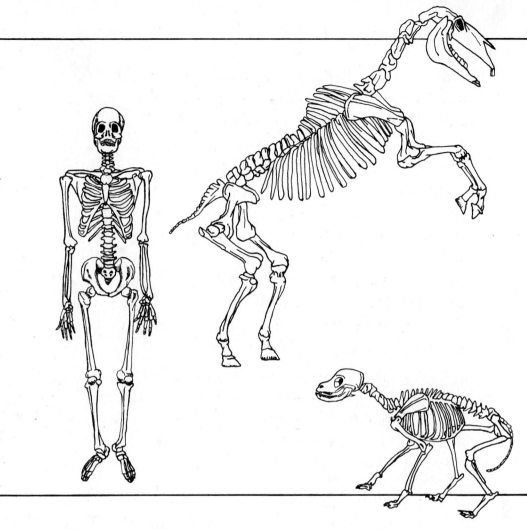

Mammals have bones

If you run your hand down your arms or legs, you can feel the bones. If you have a dog or a cat, you can feel its bones, too. All mammals have bones. The bones of an animal make up the animal's **skeleton** (skel′ə tən).

Bones hold an animal's body in shape. Bones also protect what's inside. Muscles make the bones move. Look at these skeletons. Can you see how they are alike in some ways?

skeleton
all the bones of an animal's body

Mammals have limbs

limb
an arm, a leg, a
flipper, or a wing

Mammals never have more than four **limbs,** two on each side of their backbone. Arms are limbs. So are legs. Flippers are limbs, too.

Horses stand on all four limbs. So do dogs and cats and cows. People stand on two limbs. They use their other two to hold things.

Some mammals don't stand on their limbs at all. Some mammals use their limbs for swimming. Seals use their flippers for that. So do walruses.

HOW DO YOU MOVE ON YOUR LIMBS?

Stand on one leg. How can you move?
    Stand on all four limbs. How do you move now?
    Stand on three limbs. Can you move?
    Can you walk on your hands? Can you walk on your
knees? What two limbs do you move best with?

Dolphin

Mammals breathe air

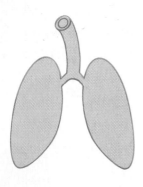

Animals need **oxygen** (ok′sə jən) to stay alive. Oxygen is a gas in the air. Mammals have lungs that take oxygen out of the air. Lungs are shaped like sacs. Your lungs are enclosed by your ribs.

Even mammals that live in the sea must come above the water to breathe. They must breathe air. They cannot take the oxygen from the water like fish do. Fish have gills to do this. Whales, otters, and other sea mammals do not have gills. They have lungs. Sea mammals would drown if they could not breathe air.

Mammals are warm-blooded

An animal's heart pumps blood to every part of its body. If a mammal is healthy, the temperature of its blood stays the same whether it is in a very hot place or a very cold place. A mammal's blood is warm.

Mammals are adapted to the places they live

adapted
fitted to a certain
way of life

Polar bears are **adapted** to the cold because they have thick coats of hair. Seals are adapted to the cold because they have layers of fat.

Gerbils live in the hot, dry desert. They are adapted to the desert because they don't need much water.

Mammals are adapted to the food they eat

All mammals are adapted to the ways they get their food and the food they eat.

A beaver has big front teeth—just right for gnawing on trees. An anteater's long nose and tongue are just right for eating ants. How is a giraffe adapted to the food it eats?

Mammals are adapted to the way they move

Some mammals walk, some run, some hop, some jump, some climb, some burrow, some swing, some fly.

A mammal moves and lives in a special way because of the ways its limbs, bones, and muscles are shaped.

Rabbits have big, strong hind legs. So do kangaroos. What could you guess about the way they move?

Gophers have very strong front legs with long claws. What could you guess about what they do?

Beavers and otters have webs between their toes. Could you guess what they can do well?

Flying mammals

One group of mammals can fly. These flying mammals are bats.

Bats have very long front limbs and fingers. A web of skin is stretched between their finger bones. This skin connects to the hind limbs, and sometimes to the tail, too. This skin allows the animal to fly.

Bats fly mostly at night. During the day they stay in caves or other dark places. When they sleep, they hang upside down.

Rodents

Some mammals have strong front teeth. These front teeth are very sharp. They are used for gnawing (nô′ing). Mammals like these are called **rodents** (rōd′nt).

Squirrels and chipmunks are rodents. So are beavers, rats, and mice.

rodent
a small mammal that uses its teeth for gnawing

Monkeys and apes

Some mammals can climb about in trees. They have hands and feet for grasping things. Monkeys and apes are like that. They have a finger or toe that sticks out at an angle from the other fingers and toes. This angled finger or toe helps the animal grasp branches and other objects.

Monkeys usually have a tail. Some monkeys, like the squirrel monkey and the howler monkey, have tails that can wrap around branches. This can help the animal climb around in trees.

Some monkeys have tails that can't wrap around branches. They have thick patches of skin on which they rest while sitting. The baboon is like that.

Apes look somewhat like monkeys. But apes don't have a tail. Their arms are usually longer than their legs. Some apes walk on their two hind legs rather than all four limbs. Gibbons are like that.

Orangutans (ô rang'ü tan') are reddish-colored apes. They live on the islands of Borneo and Sumatra.

Gorillas are apes, too. They live in the forests of western Africa. Gorillas can grow to a very large size. They weigh up to 250 kilograms (550 pounds).

Chimpanzees are apes. They are sometimes called chimps for short. Chimps look like small gorillas, but have shorter arms and a more rounded head.

An orangutan (left) and a chimpanzee with baby (below).

Hoofed mammals

hoof
the hard material
that covers the foot
of some animals

Horses are mammals. So are zebras. The feet of these animals end in one large **hoof.** The hoof is really an animal's toenail. A rhinoceros (rī nos'ər əs) is like that, too.

Some mammals have a hoof that is parted. Pigs and cows are like that. So are camels, reindeer, and giraffes. These animals walk on their toes. Animals with hooves are walking on their toes.

Sea mammals

The biggest mammals live in the sea. Grey whales, fin whales, and humpback whales are all very big. The blue whale is the biggest of all. It can grow up to 35 meters (110 feet) long. It can weigh as much as a train engine! How are such big mammals adapted for life in the sea?

Dolphins (dol′fən) and porpoises (pôr′pəs) are mammals that live in the sea, too.

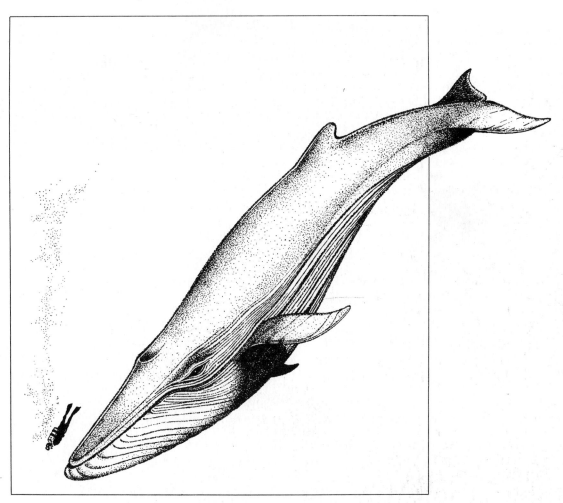

Insect-eating mammals

Mammals eat different things. Some mammals feed mainly on insects. They dig tunnels in the ground. They live in burrows. A mole is like that. So is a shrew. These animals eat other things besides insects. They are called insect-eaters because that is their main food.

Meat-eating mammals

Other mammals eat mostly meat. Cats and dogs belong in this group. So do bears and skunks and raccoons.

These animals have sharp front teeth. These long, sharp teeth are adapted to help the animals eat meat.

Some meat-eaters live in the sea. They have sharp front teeth and eat meat, too. Seals and walruses are like that.

LOOKING FOR MAMMALS

Go on a walk through the woods or in the park. Look for signs of mammals. Some of the things to look for are tracks, bits of food, holes in the ground, a little fur or hair, and droppings. Can you tell what animals made the signs that you find?

Maybe you will see some mammals. Can you find where they live? How many kinds of mammals do you see?

Pouched mammals

Some mammals have pouches. The young of these mammals grow and develop in the mother's pouch. An opossom (ə poss'əm) is like that. So is a kangaroo and a koala (kō äl'ə). These animals are **marsupials** (mär sü'pē əl).

Their babies are born alive. But the babies are very tiny—some not much bigger than a bee. When the babies are born they crawl into the pouch. There, in the pouch, the babies drink milk from the mother. When the babies can get around on their own, they come out of the pouch.

Platypus

Opossum

Some mammals lay eggs

Some mammals don't have all the mammal traits. There are a few mammals that do not give birth to live young. The platypus (plat'ə pəs) and spiny anteater are like that. They lay eggs.

A platypus and spiny anteater are still mammals. They have the other traits that mammals have. They have hair, bones, limbs, warm blood, and the mothers make milk for their young.

SCIENCE ON THE JOB

What does a farmer do when an animal gets sick? The farmer calls a veterinarian. If you have a sick pet, you might do the same thing. Another name for a veterinarian is a "vet."

Vets help to heal sick and hurt animals. They also try to prevent animals from getting sick. If you have a dog or cat, it should get regular shots. The shots help prevent certain illnesses.

Many vets specialize in small or large animals. Then they get to know more about those animals. I work with large animals. Most of my work is with horses. Taking care of horses is very interesting. Sometimes they get stomach aches like people. A horse's stomach ache is called "colic."

My car is a lab and a pharmacy. Large animals sometimes get sick. They usually can not go to the doctor. So I have to go to them.

Barbara Cunningham, V.M.D.

REVIEW QUESTIONS

1. In what ways are all mammals alike?
2. What is the first food young mammals eat?
3. What is a skeleton?
4. How do mammals that live in the sea get oxygen?
5. Why do mammals that live in cold climates grow thicker hair?
6. What does it mean to adapt?
7. What are some mammal differences?

WORDS TO REVIEW

adapt	mammal	reproduce
hoof	marsupial	rodent
limb	oxygen	skeleton

EXPLORING FURTHER

1. Find out how the teeth of plant eaters are different from the teeth of meat eaters.

2. Feel the shape of your own bones. How many ribs can you count? Feel the bones in your arm and hand. Can you find out how many bones there are in the five fingers on one hand? What other bones in your body can you feel?

3. Make a collection of animal pictures from magazines, books, or posters. Group the animals into sets with all the mammals in one set. Can you separate the animals that are mammals into several smaller sets?

4. Here are some books about mammals. You may wish to read some of them.

   THE WORLD OF CHIPPIE by Evangeline Baertsch

   THE SKELETON INSIDE YOU by Philip Balestrino

   SWIMMING MAMMALS by Susan Harris

   SQUIRRELS by George Laycock

   WONDERS OF LIONS by George and Kay Schaller

Unit 5

Our Planet Earth

What is earth made of?

How do mountains form?

Where do earthquakes

occur?

Earth is made of many things

What is earth? When you think of earth, what do you think of? Is earth the ground under your feet?

When most people think of earth, they think of soil. They think of rocks. They think of something solid.

But earth is made of many things. It is made of solids, liquids, and gases. It has trees and rocks. It has air and oceans. It has you and me.

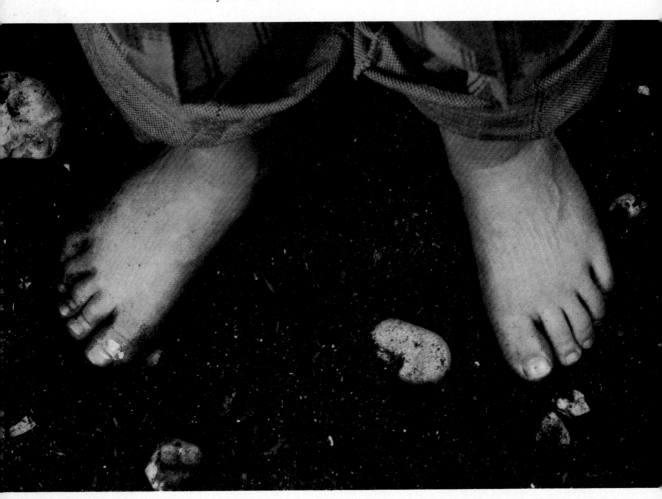

Air is part of earth

Air is part of earth. The air is wrapped around earth like a blanket. Earth's blanket of air is called the **atmosphere** (at'məs fir).

The atmosphere is a mixture of gases. There is oxygen, carbon dioxide, and nitrogen. These are only three of the many gases in the air.

Breathe in. Take air into your lungs. Every day you breathe in about 14 kilograms (30 pounds) of earth's air.

Water is part of earth

Do you swim in a lake or the ocean? Have you fished in rivers and streams? Oceans, lakes, rivers and streams are part of earth. The waters in ponds and swamps are part of earth, too. You can see earth's water in clouds. You feel earth's water when it rains.

There is water in the ground, too. Most of earth's fresh liquid water is in the ground. When it rains, water goes into the soil. The water moves down into the spaces between the soil particles. Water below the surface of earth is called **ground water.**

ground water
water below the surface of earth

Some of earth's water is frozen. Does it snow where you live? In some places the snow never melts. The snow piles up, year after year. This piled up snow forms icy **glaciers** (glā′shər).

Some glaciers cover land near the ocean. Large pieces of these glaciers may break off. They fall into the ocean and slowly float away. These floating pieces of glacier are called **icebergs.**

Icebergs can be very large pieces of glacier. The largest iceberg known was 332 kilometers (208 miles) long. It was 96 kilometers (60 miles) wide. That's bigger than the entire state of Maryland!

glacier
large mass of ice, formed from snow, that moves slowly downhill

iceberg
a mass of ice broken away from a glacier and floating in the ocean

129

Rocks are part of earth

Earth's land is covered by a very thin layer of soil. This is the part of solid earth you know best. If you dig down through the soil, sooner or later you will find rock.

Sometimes you see rocks at earth's surface. Rock is under your feet even when you can't see it. We call the hard rock earth's **crust.**

crust
earth's outer layer of rock

All over earth, the surface looks different. In some places there are fields and woods. Cities cover some of earth's surface. But most of earth's surface is covered by water. Under the fields and woods and cities, earth's crust is made of rock. The rocky crust is under the oceans, too.

The shape of earth

Long ago, people had different ideas about what the earth was like. Some people thought earth was floating on an ocean inside a mountain. They thought the sun and the moon hung from the roof inside the mountain.

In India, people thought earth was a giant bowl carried by elephants. When the elephants moved, the earth shook. People thought this was what caused earthquakes.

Other people thought that earth was flat. If you walked or sailed far enough, they thought you would fall off the edge of earth.

But now we know the earth is a **sphere** (sfir). A ball is a sphere. A balloon is a sphere. A soap bubble is a sphere, too. A sphere is round. Earth is shaped like a sphere.

sphere
a round object

133

Earth's crust

All the dry land on earth is part of the crust. The big land areas are called **continents.** You live on the continent of North America. Can you find North America on a map? Can you find it on a globe? Can you put your finger on the other continents?

A big part of all the continents is made of a rock called **granite** (gran′it).

The land at the bottom of the ocean is part of the crust, too. Under the oceans, the crust is made mostly of a kind of heavy, dark rock called **basalt** (bə sôlt′).

continent
one of the big land areas of the world

granite
a very hard rock making up most of earth's dry land

basalt
a dark rock making up earth's crust under the oceans

granite

basalt

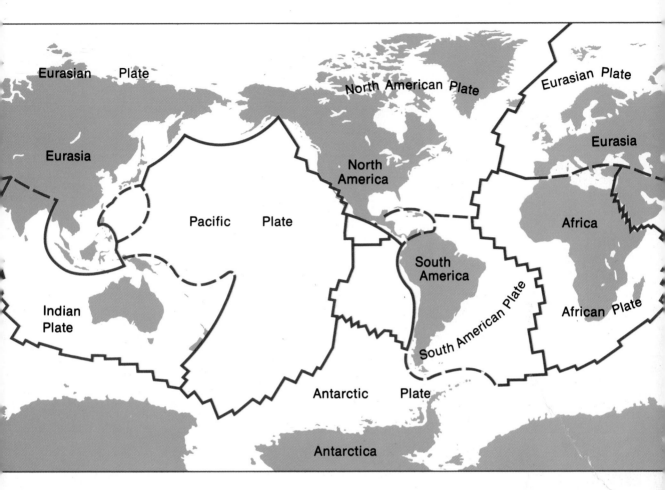

Earth's crust is broken

Earth's crust is broken into large pieces. These pieces are called **plates.** Earth's plates are about 32 kilometers (20 miles) thick.

    In the picture, the lines that separate the plates are easy to see. Trace the outline of the Pacific Plate.

    The line separating two plates is usually on the ocean floor. But sometimes it is on dry land. The San Andreas Fault is an example of this. This **fault** is in California.

plate
large piece of the earth's crust

fault
a break in earth's crust

*A rock
"floats" on
toothpaste*

Earth's crust is moving

Earth's plates move. They move very, very slowly. It may take a whole year for a plate to move about two centimeters (one inch).

How do these plates move? Scientists think there is liquid rock below earth's crust. They think earth's plates are floating on this liquid.

All liquids are not like water. Honey is a liquid. When you pour honey, it flows, but very slowly. Molasses is a liquid. It flows even slower than honey. Toothpaste is a liquid, too. Think about how slowly toothpaste flows.

The liquid that the earth's plates float on is very thick. It is thicker than toothpaste. The heavy earth plates can float on this liquid because it is so thick.

Where two plates meet

There is a lot of activity at the edges of earth's plates. Some plates are moving together. **Earthquakes** occur here. An earthquake is a sudden movement of earth's crust.

   Some plates are moving apart. **Volcanoes** may occur here. This volcano lies at the edge of plates that are moving apart. A volcano forms when hot liquids and other material rush out to earth's surface.

   Some plates are sliding past each other. These plates may move quickly. If they do, then there is an earthquake. The American Plate and the Pacific Plate are rubbing together in California. They are rubbing together at the San Andreas Fault.

earthquake
a sudden movement of earth's crust

volcano
a mountain built by outpourings of liquid rock, fine dust, and pieces of solid rock

HOW DO EARTHQUAKES HAPPEN?

Put your hands together. Press them together very hard. Now open your hands. Place them on your face. How do your hands feel? Do they feel warm? The pressure of your hands caused heat.

Press your hands together again. Press very hard. Now try to slide your hands. Do they slide easily? When your hands slide, do they move slowly or in one sudden motion?

If your hands were earth plates, what would the sudden sliding motion be called?

Earth changes

What does earth look like where you live? In some places there are rolling hills. But they didn't always look like that. Once, long, long ago, these hills may have been sharp, high mountains.

In some places there are sharp, high mountains. But these mountains weren't always there. Once, long, long ago, the rock of these mountains was at the bottom of the sea.

The crust of earth is always changing. Some changes are fast. Weather changes the earth's surface. A flood may wash away the soil. A **hurricane** (hėr′ə kān) is a storm with heavy rains and strong winds. A hurricane can wash away a beach.

hurricane
storm with heavy rains and strong winds

Some earth changes start deep inside earth. They change earth's surface, too. Islands can be formed from volcanoes. Volcanoes and earthquakes make mountains, too.

But most earth changes take a long, long time. Earth changes may take millions of years.

139

Mississippi River delta region. The aerial photo shows how sediment carried by the river settles out in a fan shape where the river enters the ocean.

Grand Canyon

Water changes earth

Look at the sidewalk after a rain storm. Do you find mud? Raindrops moved the soil onto the walk. In places where there are no plants, rain can move a lot of soil.

Water in rivers and streams moves soil, too. The faster the stream moves, the more soil it can carry. It carries the soil down to the sea.

Water wears away rock. Moving water can cut into a mountain. This happens every day. But rocks change very, very slowly. It took millions of years for the Grand Canyon to be formed.

Ice changes earth

Have you ever put a container filled with water into a freezer? If you have, the container may have broken. As the water froze, it expanded. The ice took up more space than the water did. The expanded ice made the container crack.

When water freezes on earth's surface, it can expand and crack rocks. This breaks the rocks into smaller and smaller pieces. This wears the rocks down. Ice changes the surface of earth slowly.

Ice can change earth's surface in another way. Ice can help rub the earth smooth.

Glaciers that form in the mountains flow slowly downhill. As a glacier moves, it picks up boulders and pebbles. The moving ice, and the boulders and pebbles in it, rub at the earth like a giant piece of sandpaper. This changes the surface of earth by rounding out valleys.

Wind changes earth

Have you ever seen leaves and paper blown by the wind? Wind picks them up and moves them.

Wind moves sand and soil, too. The wind-blown sand acts like sandpaper, smoothing and carving earth's surface.

When the wind slows down, it drops the sand and soil. If enough sand grains are dropped, sand dunes may form.

143

Earth is built up

Water wears down earth's crust. Ice can crack rock into small pieces. Wind and glaciers wear earth's surface smooth. Why hasn't the earth worn away?

In 1943 a volcano erupted from a flat corn field in Mexico. This volcano changed earth's surface. It built up a mountain.

Sometimes volcanoes are very large. They can spew out materials from more than one place. These kinds of volcanoes can form more than one mountain.

When volcanoes erupt under the sea, islands can be formed. Many islands are the tops of undersea mountains. Sometimes more than one undersea volcano erupts to form more than one island. A whole chain of islands might be formed. Curving chains of islands formed in this way are called **island arcs.** The Aleutian (ə lü′shən) Islands near Alaska were formed that way. Can you see the curving chain formed by these islands in the picture?

island arc
curving chain of
volcanic islands

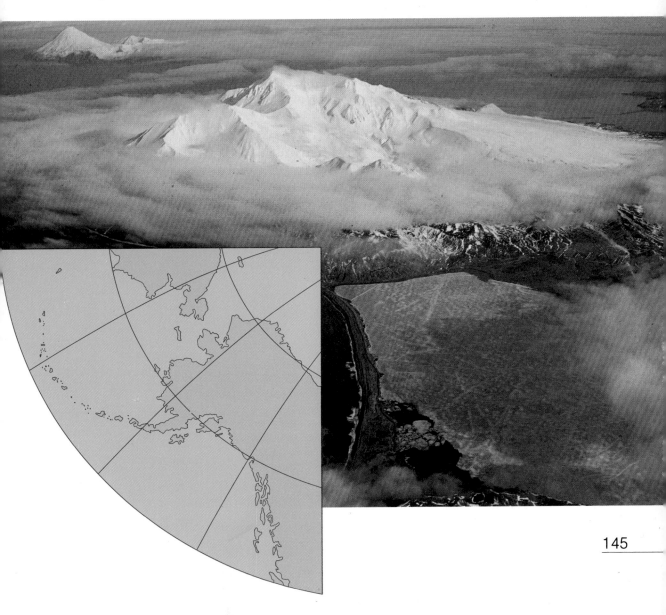

But mountains can form in another way. Think about earth's plates that are moving toward each other. These huge pieces of earth's crust are pressing against each other with great pressure. This great pressure can cause earth's plates to bend. If they bend upward, mountains may be formed. The Appalachian (ap′ə lā′chən) Mountains were formed that way. These mountains are in the eastern United States. They stretch from Canada to Alabama.

Place several sheets of different colored paper in a neat stack. With your fingertips, push from each end of the paper stack. What happens to the paper? What does the paper stack represent? What do your pushing fingers represent? What does the shape of the pushed paper represent? Does this process take longer when rocks are being pushed instead of paper?

How could you get more than one mountain to form?

Place a long rug flat on the floor. Push the rug from one end and have another student push from the other end. What happens? If the rug were earth's surface, what would the ripples in the rug be called?

147

Mountains come in all shapes and sizes. Some are tall and pointed. Some are low and rounded. The tallest mountain on earth's dry land is Mt. Everest. It is more than 9 kilometers (5.5 miles) tall.

Mt. McKinley is in Alaska. It is the tallest mountain in the western United States. It is more than 6 kilometers (3.8 miles) tall.

The tallest mountain in the eastern United States is Mt. Mitchell. This mountain is in North Carolina. It is 2 kilometers (1.2 miles) high.

Valleys

Mountains are the high spots on earth's crust. But there are low spots, too.

Some low areas are called **valleys.** Valleys are the low places between mountains or hills. The lowest valley in the United States is Death Valley. It stretches from eastern California to southern Nevada. Death Valley is 85 meters (280 feet) below sea level.

The tallest mountain on earth would fit into the deepest trench.

Trenches

There are low places under the ocean, too. A low place in the ocean floor is called a **trench.** A trench is found where earth plates come together on the ocean floor. Trenches are much deeper than any valley on dry land.

trench
long, narrow depression on the ocean floor

The deepest trench is found in the Pacific Ocean near Japan. It is more than 10 kilometers (almost 7 miles) deep. Mt. Everest, the tallest mountain on dry land, would fit inside this trench. It would still be under water.

These people are washing and examining dredge samples from beneath the ocean.

How we learn about earth

We know many things about the inside of earth. But nobody has ever seen inside earth. We learn through instruments that measure earthquakes and volcanoes. We learn by studying the hot liquid that comes through a volcano. We learn by studying the crust where earth's plates meet.

Scientists from all over the world are studying earth. Sometimes they work alone. Sometimes they come together to study. Here, scientists from the United States, France, and Mexico are studying deep below the ocean. They are studying what happens where earth's plates meet. From these studies we will learn more about earth.

SCIENCE ON THE JOB

The earth around us is always changing. You have read about some of the ways this happens. People change the earth, too. Roads, buildings, and landscapes change. Boundaries between properties must be marked.

Surveyors measure and mark boundaries. These boundaries are then recorded. New land owners can find the exact boundaries of their property.

Surveyors also help map makers. They check the distances between places. Survey maps also show the heights of the land areas.

REVIEW QUESTIONS

1. What is the atmosphere?
2. How is a glacier formed?
3. What is earth's crust?
4. Is earth's crust all one piece? Explain.
5. What happens where two earth plates meet?
6. Name three things that can change the surface of the earth.
7. What is an earthquake?
8. What are two ways that mountains can form?

WORDS TO REVIEW

atmosphere	earthquake	groundwater	plate
basalt	fault	hurricane	sphere
continent	glacier	iceberg	trench
crust	granite	island arc	valley
			volcano

EXPLORING FURTHER

1. Tar and pitch are liquids, somewhat like the liquid material under earth's plates. Try to get a blob of tar. Put it in a jar cap or an old dish. Does the tar change shape after several weeks?

2. Put plaster of paris in a can. When it is almost dry, plant a dry seed in it. Set the hardened plaster in a cup of water. What does the seed do to the plaster rock?

3. Find out how sandpaper is made. How is using sandpaper to smooth a piece of wood like wind-blown sand smoothing rocks?

4. Ask an older person to help you melt some things in the oven. Let the oven heat up to 500°F. Then put in different substances on an aluminum pan. Try some salt, sugar, plastic, wood, metal, soap, solder, and a rock. Guess which things will change and which will stay the same. Look in the oven after 15 minutes to see what happened.

5. You may want to learn more about earth. Here are some books about earth you could read.

    ICEBERG ALLEY by Madelyn Klein Anderson

    A BOOK OF PLANET EARTH FOR YOU by Franklyn M. Branley

    OUR FRAGILE EARTH by E. S. Helfman

    PLANET EARTH by Christopher Maynard

    EARTHQUAKES: OUR RESTLESS PLANET by Margaret Reuter

    LANDS ADRIFT: THE STORY OF THE CONTINENTAL DRIFT by Malcolm E. Weiss

Unit 6
Force

How does an airplane stay up?

What makes lightning?

Why do things fall down

instead of up?

What makes things move?

There are many ways to move objects. You can throw a ball. A horse can pull a wagon. The wind can move a sailboat. Can you think of other ways to move things?

What can stop a moving object? A player can catch the ball. The horse can stop pulling the wagon. The wind can become calm. Can you think of other ways to stop moving things?

Objects don't just start moving by themselves. Something is needed to get them started. That something is called a **force.** Then the objects will keep on moving until they are stopped by something. That something is a force, too. Force is a push or a pull that changes the motion of an object. A force can start a thing moving. A force can stop a moving thing.

Force is needed to pull a wagon or turn the wheels of a bicycle. Force is needed to stop a car or catch a ball.

What makes moving objects change their direction?

When a force starts an object moving, the object will move in a straight line. But sometimes moving objects change their direction. It takes a force to do that. A force is needed to change the direction of a moving object.

Leaves blow in a different direction if the wind shifts. The direction of a moving ball is changed if it hits a bat. What can change the direction of a toy car? What can change the direction of a rowboat?

159

Sit on the floor about 2 meters in front of a partner. Roll a ball to your partner. What did you do to the ball to start it moving? What kind of path did the ball take? What made the ball stop moving?

Now have your partner roll the ball back to you. Can you change the direction of the rolling ball? How many ways can you do this?

What starts an object moving? In what direction do objects move? What does it take to change a moving object's direction? What is needed to stop a moving object?

What makes a moving object change speed?

Sometimes when an object is moving, something happens to change its speed. You can change the speed of your bike by pedaling faster or slower. You can change the speed of a sled by moving your weight or by dragging your foot.

Think of some other ways to change the speed of a moving object. Can you tell what force has acted?

Whenever an object speeds up, a force is acting on it. The more force you apply to an object, the faster it will go. Whenever an object slows down, a force is acting on it. The more force applied to the object, the sooner it will slow down.

CHANGING THE SPEED OF A MOVING OBJECT

Roll two equal-sized balls to a partner. Make one roll very quickly. Make one roll more slowly. Which ball did you push harder? Your "push" is a force. What can you say about the amount of force needed to make an object move faster?

Now have a friend roll the two balls toward you. One ball should roll very quickly. The other ball should roll very slowly. Stop the rolling balls with your hands. Which ball needed more force to be stopped?

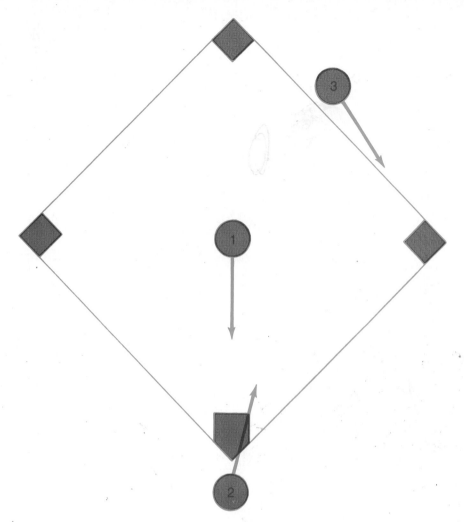

Showing forces

You can draw a picture of what happened in the activities. To show a force acting on a ball, draw an arrow. This arrow is called a **vector.** The vector should point in the direction of the force. If the force is great, the vector can be long. If the force is small, use a short vector.

vector
an arrow that shows the amount and direction of a force

Here is a force drawing. Look at the vectors. Can you tell what is happening?

Earth's force

When you drop a ball, you don't have to think about which direction it will fall. You know it will fall downward.

What force pulls it down? You could call it earth force. The name for earth force is **gravity** (grav'ə tē). Earth's gravity pulls everything toward the center of earth. We call this direction "down."

Earth's gravity pulls on things everywhere on earth—on the surface of the earth, in the air above earth, and even on things above the air.

That's why things never fall up. "Up" is another way of saying, "Out, away from the center of earth." Up is out or away from earth's center. Down is in, toward the center.

If you coast down a hill on your bike, it is gravity that pulls you down. But when you start to go up a hill, you have to move against gravity. To ride your bike all the way up the hill, you need to overcome the force of gravity.

A rocket engine pushes a spacecraft up. Gravity pulls the spacecraft down. The force of the rocket engine must be greater than the force of gravity for the rocket to go up.

Nothing goes up or comes down by itself. Some force has to push it up. Some force has to pull it down.

Sometimes the forces pushing and pulling on an object are equal. When that happens, the object won't start moving.

When you hold a book, the amount of muscle force you are using to hold it up is the same as the amount of gravity force pulling it down. The book doesn't move. What would happen to the book if the gravity force were greater than your muscle force?

A block of wood floats because the amount of water force pushing it up is the same as the amount of gravity force pulling it down. What would happen if the gravity force pulling on the wood were greater than the water force pushing it up?

Heavy and light

Earth's gravity pulls harder on some things than it does on others. When gravity pulls harder, we say the thing is heavier.

Sometimes it's easy to tell if gravity is pulling harder on one thing than on another. You can tell by lifting the thing. A brick is heavier than a coin. The brick presses down harder on your hand. So you know that gravity is pulling harder on the brick than on the coin.

Sometimes you can't tell which thing is heavier by just lifting. Is an apple heavier than an orange? You can't be sure until you weigh them. You use a scale to measure how much gravity pulls on something. **Weight** tells how much gravity force is pulling on an object. It measures the force of gravity.

How much do you weigh? When we ask this, we are really asking, "How strong is gravity pulling on you?" Let's say you weigh half as much as another person. The force of earth's gravity on you is half that of the other person.

weight
the amount of gravity pulling on an object

167

Magnetic force

Have you ever used a magnet? Magnets come in many shapes and sizes. They can be circles, bars or horseshoes. Some of them are U-shaped. Most magnets are made of iron. Magnets all have one thing in common. They all put out a force. This force is called **magnetic force.** Magnetic force can pull or push.

magnetic force
the push or pull of a magnet

magnetic pole
a place on a magnet where its force seems to be strongest

Magnets have areas called **magnetic poles.** Usually the poles are at the ends of the magnet. Most of a magnet's force is at its poles. A magnet has an N-pole and an S-pole.

Earth is like a magnet too. Earth has magnetic poles. One magnetic pole is near the top of earth. It is called the north magnetic pole. The other pole is near the bottom of earth. It is called the south magnetic pole.

MAGNETS

Collect many kinds of objects. Find a pencil, a penny, paper clips, cork, paper, aluminum foil, glass, and some other objects. Try to pick up each object with a magnet. Which of the things does a magnet pick up?

Put some paper clips in a pile. Touch the magnet to the paper clips. Does the magnet pick up the clips? Where do the paper clips cling to the magnet? Are there more clips on some parts of the magnet? If more clips cling to the magnet in certain areas, these are the magnetic poles.

Put two bar magnets end-to-end about 2 centimeters (1 inch) apart. What happens? Slowly move them closer together. What happens?

Now turn one of the magnets around. Again move them closer together. What happens?

What can you say about the poles of magnets?

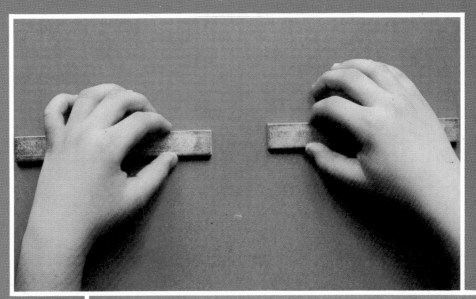

Magnets attract and repel

The N-pole of one magnet will pull toward the S-pole of another magnet. The two poles **attract** (ə trakt′). Poles that are different, attract.

The S-poles of two magnets push away, or **repel** (ri pel′), each other. Poles that are alike, repel.

A compass depends on magnetic force to show direction. The needle in a compass is a small magnet. It is attracted to earth's magnetic poles. When you use a compass, earth's magnetic force acts on the needle. The needle points to earth's north magnetic pole.

attract
to pull close together

repel
to push away

171

Magnetic fields

Magnetic force goes out into the space around a magnet. This is called a **magnetic field.** You cannot see a magnetic field. To picture a magnetic field in your mind, think of curved lines that connect the north and south poles of a magnet. Where the magnet is strongest, the lines are closer together. The lines are farthest apart where the magnet is weaker. These curved lines are called **lines of force.**

magnetic field
the space around a magnet where its magnetic force can be detected

lines of force
imaginary curved lines connecting the north and south poles of a magnet

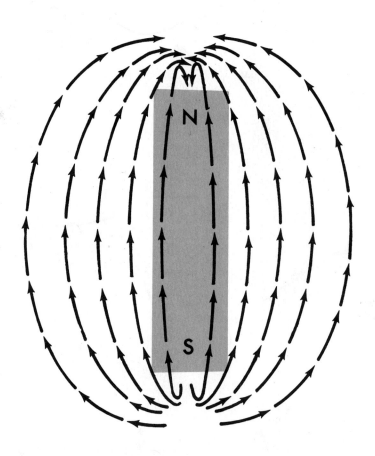

Rest a bar magnet flat on a table. Cover the magnet with a sheet of white paper. Sprinkle iron filings on the paper. What happens to the iron filings? Do you see a pattern? Make a drawing of the iron filings.

Now do the very same thing with a different kind of magnet. Make a drawing of the iron filings now.

Look at both drawings. What do the patterns show?

The force of air and wind

Have you ever watched a sailboat moving on a lake? Have you seen a line of wet clothes flapping in the breeze or a pinwheel whirling around? These things move because of the wind. Moving air, or wind, has force.

On a windy day, you can feel the force on your face. It might even blow papers out of your hand. Wind pushes against sails and makes a sailboat move. If the wind is blowing hard, the boat goes fast. On a calm day, with little wind, a sailboat moves slowly. The more wind force, the faster the sailboat moves. Can you make a vector drawing of a sailboat race?

Air has force even if it's not moving. It pushes on everything. Air has push, or force, because air has weight. This push of air is called **air pressure.**

You might ask, "If air has pressure, why don't we feel it?" There is air inside your body. The air is pushing outward. The air outside your body is pushing inward. Air in your body pushes outward with as much force as the outside air pushing inward. The forces are equal.

air pressure
the pushing force of air

Have you ever wondered how airplanes can fly? Gravity pulls an airplane down. Air pressure pushes it up. If the force of air pushing up is greater, the airplane is lifted. Then the air pressure on the bottom of the wing is greater than the pressure on the top.

The pressure is greater when the wing is moved through the air. If the wing moves fast enough, the upward force is greater than the downward force of gravity. This is called the take-off. Can you figure out how an airplane lands?

Fill a glass with water. Make sure the water comes to the very top. As you fill the glass, what happens to the air in the glass? Now cover the top of the glass with a piece of thin cardboard.

Do this next part carefully. Do it over a pail in case of a spill. Keep one hand flat on the cardboard and quickly turn the glass upside down. Slowly remove your hand from the cardboard.

The water is pushing down. Air is pushing up. Why doesn't the cardboard fall?

A cement surface has lots of small bumps and valleys.

A force that slows things down

Whenever two things move against each other, there is **friction.** Friction is a force that slows down moving objects.

When smooth surfaces rub against each other, there is less friction than if the surfaces are rough. A smooth, wood floor has hardly any bumps on it.

But if you feel a cement sidewalk with your fingers, you will feel a lot of bumps. If you look at it through a hand lens you can see the bumps, like little mountains and valleys. Which surface would have more force to push something back?

The bumpier and rougher surfaces are, the more friction there is.

friction
a force that slows down moving objects

179

When something moves through the air or water, there is friction, too. Air has friction. If you wave a piece of cardboard through the air, you can feel the force. Water friction slows down swimmers and boats.

Friction is also helpful. Without friction you would have a hard time walking. If the sidewalk is covered with ice, what happens? What can be done to make the ice have more friction? How does a bicycle brake use friction?

Friction causes heat. Rub your hands together back and forth. Do you feel the heat? If you rub a piece of wood with sandpaper, the wood will get smooth. But something else happens. The wood and sandpaper get warm.

The moving parts of many machines rub against each other. There is friction. It causes heat. That is why machines need oil. Oil is a smooth liquid. It keeps the parts from wearing away. It also keeps the machine parts from getting too hot.

Static electricity

Have you ever scuffed across a rug, then tingled when you touched something? Did you hear a faint crackling sound? Did you see a spark?

These things were caused by **static electricity.** Static electricity is a force produced by friction or rubbing. When you rub one object with another you make electricity. The electricity can jump from one object to another. This is why you feel the shock when you touch something. When air and clouds "scuff" during a storm, you see the spark as lightning. Static electricity as lightning has a lot of force. Take care during storms to protect yourself from lightning.

Current electricity

When electricity flows, we call it **current electricity.** This force can light a lamp, heat a toaster, or ring a telephone. Current electricity can travel through wires.

The wires are made in a path called a **circuit** (sėr'kit). To work, however, the circuit must not have any spaces or gaps in it. The electricity must have an unbroken path to follow.

When all the parts of a circuit are connected, we say the circuit is closed. Electricity can flow through all parts of the circuit. It has no spaces or gaps.

If all the parts of the circuit are not connected, the circuit is open. The electricity cannot flow through all parts of the circuit. So the electricity stops. Opening a circuit on purpose allows us to control the flow.

current electricity
electricity flowing through a wire

circuit
a path through which electricity flows

183

MAKING AN ELECTRICAL CIRCUIT

Cut a piece of copper wire about 30 centimeters (12 inches) long. Wrap one end of the wire once around the base of a small flashlight bulb.

Touch the free end of the wire to the flat bottom of a flashlight battery. Touch the small metal bead on the bottom of the bulb to the post on the top of the battery. What happens?

Are there any gaps or spaces in the circuit you just made? What kind of circuit has no gaps or spaces? What happens to electrical current in this kind of circuit?

Now take the wire end away from the battery. What happens to the light bulb? Why?

What kind of circuit has gaps or spaces? What happens to the electric current in this kind of circuit?

Can you make the light bulb go on and off? How is this like a light switch in your home?

SCIENCE ON THE JOB

Did you ever wonder how a telephone works? A telephone uses electrical force and magnetic force.

Telephone workers have different kinds of jobs. An operator helps people by finding numbers. Some workers make telephones. Others install them. Still others make repairs or hang wires.

Some telephone calls travel through space! But a telephone wouldn't work without force.

REVIEW QUESTIONS

1. What is force?
2. What is the force that pulls everything toward the center of earth?
3. Name some things that are slowed down by the friction of air.
4. What kinds of objects do magnets pick up or attract?
5. Where is a magnet usually strongest? What are these places called?
6. What causes lightning?
7. You flip a switch to make the lights turn on in a room. What did the light switch do to the circuit to make the lights go on?

WORDS TO REVIEW

air pressure	force	magnetic pole
attract	friction	repel
circuit	gravity	static electricity
current electricity	magnetic force	vector
		weight

EXPLORING FURTHER

1. Toss a ball into the air. Tell what happens to it. Use the words up, down, force, speed, move, direction.

2. Drop a sheet of paper and watch it fall to the floor. What happens to it? Tell how it falls. What slows it down? Crumple the piece of paper. Drop it again. How does it fall this time? Can you make the paper fall faster?

3. Turn on the water faucet so a small, steady stream flows out. Comb your hair with a rubber comb. Hold the comb near the stream of water. What happens? What force is acting?

4. You can make a compass with a magnet. Tie a 30-centimeter (12-inch) piece of thin thread to a bar magnet. Tie one end of the string to one end of the magnet, and the other end of the string to the other end of the magnet. Hang the magnet from a hook. Make sure the magnet is level, and swings freely. Allow the magnet to stop turning. What position is it in? Does it point north or south? Compare it with the needle of a compass.

5. Fold square pieces of paper to make airplanes. Make one airplane with a pointed nose, and one plane with a blunt or square nose. Try to make both of them fly across the room. Which plane flies farther? Does the shape of the airplane affect the way it flies? Why does the pointed airplane fly farther through the air before it stops?

6. Find out how a telephone works. Ask someone who knows about telephones to explain it to you. Then make a report to the class.

7. Here are some books you might like to read.

CATCH THE WIND: A BOOK OF WINDPOWER by Landt Dennis

WHY KITES FLY: THE STORY OF THE WIND AT WORK by Don Dwiggins

SAVING ELECTRICITY by Sam and Beryl Epstein

FORCES IN THE EARTH: GRAVITY AND MAGNETISM by R. J. Lefkowitz

SILENT WINGS: EXPERIMENTING WITH PAPER AIRPLANES AND BALSA GLIDERS by Kristine Cox Levine

190

Unit 7

Plant and Animal Cells

What are cells? Do you have any?

Do you have "your mother's eyes"

or "your father's smile"?

Do plants have eggs?

Many, many cells

Look around you. Look at the living things. Look at frogs and cats and ants. Look at trees and flowers and grass. All living things are made of tiny parts. These tiny parts are called **cells.**

Large plants and animals are made of billions of cells. A tree is a plant made of billions of cells. A monkey is an animal made of billions of cells. Some living things are made of only one cell.

cell
building blocks of living things.

Size and shape

All cells are not alike. Cells come in different sizes. They come in different shapes. Some cells are very, very small. They are so small you can see them only when you look through a microscope. There are some very big cells, too. A hen's egg is one big cell.

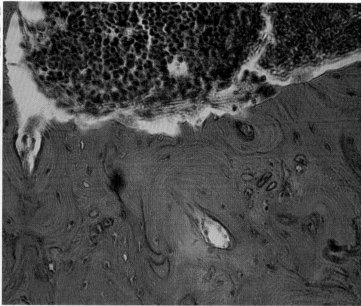

bone cells

muscle cells

Different kinds of cells

Look at your finger. There are millions of cells there. The ones you see are skin cells. Bend your finger. Muscle cells are at work. They make your finger move. Feel the bones in your finger. Your bones are made of bone cells.

You are made of many different kinds of cells. Different kinds of cells do different jobs. Dogs and robins and sunflowers are made of different kinds of cells, too. Different kinds of cells are the building blocks of all living things.

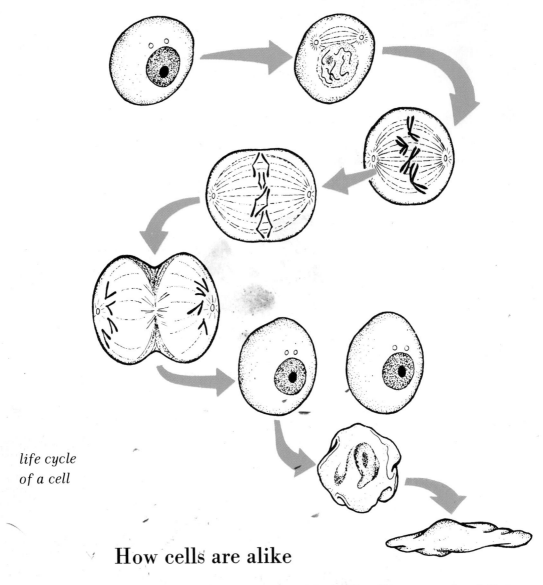

*life cycle
of a cell*

How cells are alike

In some ways all cells are alike. All cells are made of living stuff. They take in food. Cells can grow. Oxygen goes into every cell.

Cells change food into more living stuff. They break down food to make energy. Cells reproduce. They make more cells. Then, sooner or later, the cells die.

A closer look

Suppose you looked through a microscope at a drop of your blood.

What would you see? Cells. What would you see if you looked at the skin of a frog? Cells. What would you see if you looked at a piece of onion? Cells.

Each cell is different. But in some ways, the cells are alike. Plant and animal cells are alike in many ways.

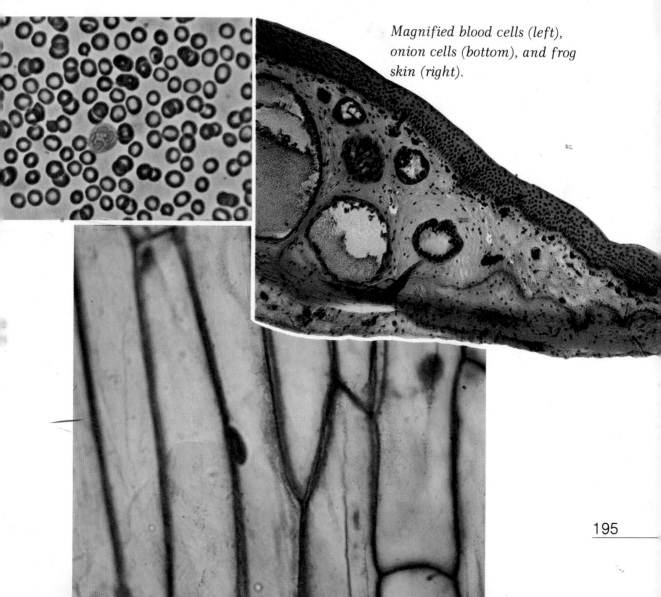

Magnified blood cells (left), onion cells (bottom), and frog skin (right).

Parts of cells

Look closely at each cell. Each cell has a dark spot. This spot is called the **nucleus** (nū′klē əs).

Around each cell is a very thin skin. This skin is called the **cell membrane.** Each cell is enclosed in this membrane.

The membrane keeps the liquid in the cell together. This liquid is called the **cytoplasm** (sīt′ə plaz′ əm). All cells are made up of a nucleus, a cell membrane, and cytoplasm.

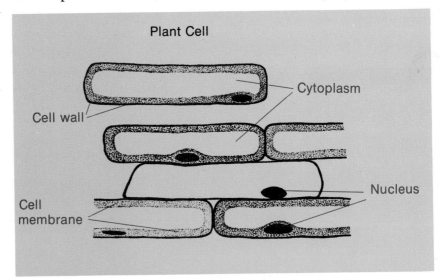

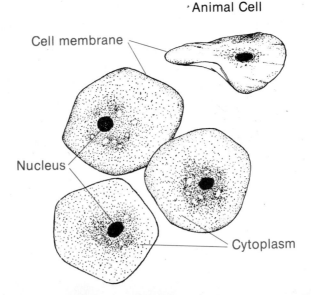

What cell parts do

The nucleus is an important part of the cell. Without a nucleus cells can't reproduce. A cell without a nucleus can't even stay alive. The living stuff inside the nucleus is held together by another membrane. This membrane is called the **nuclear** (nü′klē ər) **membrane.**

Cytoplasm is the cell material outside the nucleus. The cytoplasm is a busy place. Have you ever watched soup boiling? That's how the cytoplasm looks when you look at it through a microscope.

Food comes into the cell through the cell membrane. It lets other things pass out of the cell. Oxygen goes into the cell through the cell membrane. Wastes pass out through the cell membrane.

nuclear membrane
thin lining which encloses a cell nucleus

A MODEL OF A CELL MEMBRANE

A cell membrane lets some things pass into the cell. It lets other things out. You can make a model of a cell membrane.

Pour about $\frac{1}{4}$ cup of starch solution into a plastic bag. Make a ball of clay about the size of a pea. Drop the clay into the bag. Close the bag with a twist tie. This is a model of a cell.

Half-fill a glass with warm water. Add a few drops of iodine solution to the water. Add iodine until the water turns a light rust color.

Place the cell model in the glass. Be sure the cell model is covered with the iodine water.

Watch the liquid inside the cell. Is it changing color? Watch the liquid outside the cell. Is it changing color?

The liquid inside the cell changes color. It becomes blue-black. Iodine makes starch turn blue-black. If the liquid inside the cell turns blue-black, you know that the iodine outside the cell has passed through the membrane. The iodine is now inside the cell.

In a real cell, food passes in through the cell membrane. Wastes pass out through the membrane.

A LOOK AT SOME ONION CELLS

Look at different onion cells through a microscope. Your teacher can help you make the slides. Make a slide of a thin piece of onion skin. Then make a slide of a thin slice of onion leaf. What do these onion cells look like?

First, look at the leaf cells. Inside each cell are tiny green dots. These are the chloroplasts. Then look at the onion skin slide. There are no chloroplasts there.

In some ways the onion cells are alike. They have differences, too. How are the cells alike? How are they different? What do you see?

Over and over again

Every living thing produces similar living things. Animals make new animals like themselves. Plants make new plants like themselves. When something is passed from parent to offspring, we say it is **inherited.**

inherit
to receive a trait from parents

Every living thing inherits **traits** from its parents. A trait is something that describes the way you are. The color of your hair is a trait. Your height and the color of your eyes are traits, too.

trait
a characteristic inherited from parents

All of your traits came from your parents and grandparents. They came from your great-grandparents, too. You inherited these traits through your cells.

What will it be?

Every cell of every living thing has traits that decide what that living thing will be like. The traits even decide what each cell will be like. **Heredity** (hə red′ə tē) is all the traits a cell gets from its parent cells.

A rose is a rose because of its heredity. Whether it is red or pink or yellow, even how it smells, depends on its heredity.

You are you because of your heredity. Your skin is light or dark, your eyes are brown or blue, your hair is straight or curly because of the traits you inherited from your parents.

heredity
all the traits a cell or organism gets from its parents

From one cell

Every living thing starts as a single cell. A giant redwood tree starts as a single cell. The cell grows into a seed. An elephant starts as a single cell. The egg cell is in its mother's body.

From one parent

The simplest kinds of living things are made of just one cell. They reproduce by dividing in two. One **amoeba** (ə mē′ bə) becomes two amoebas. A one-celled **alga** (al′gə) becomes two algae (al′ jē).

amoeba
tiny, one-celled animal

amoeba dividing

two amoebas

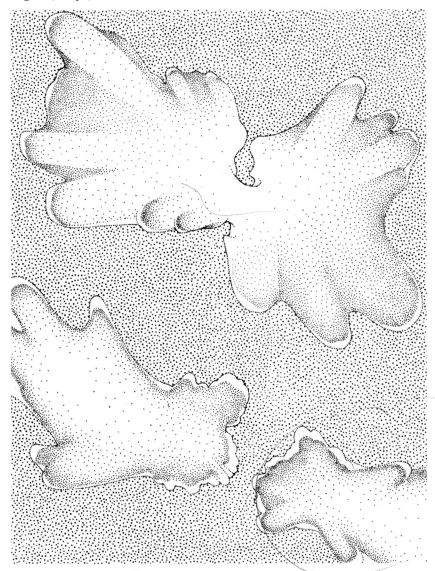

Yeast cells budding

Some simple living things reproduce by **budding.** Yeast cells reproduce this way. As the yeast cell grows, part of it pushes out through the cell wall. When this part is a complete cell, it breaks off. Then there are two yeast cells.

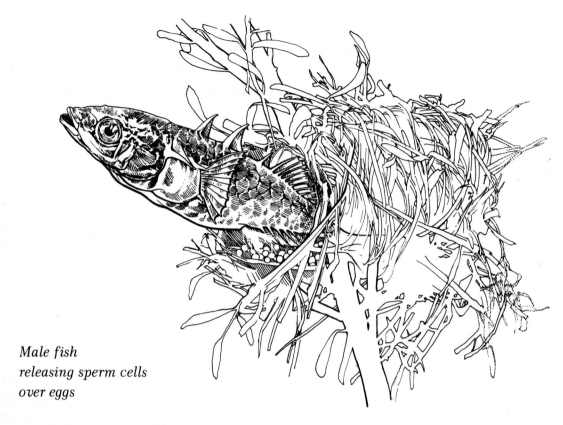

*Male fish
releasing sperm cells
over eggs*

Two parents

Some plants and animals reproduce when two special cells come together. One kind is a **sperm cell.** Sperm cells are usually very, very small. They come from the male.

The other kind of cell is an **egg cell.** Egg cells are usually much larger than the sperm cells. Egg cells come from the female.

Egg cells usually stay in one place, but the sperm cells can move about. When the sperm cell and the egg cell come together, they form a new cell. This new cell divides and grows. It divides, changes, and develops until it becomes a new plant or animal with many cells.

Seeds start as eggs

Most kinds of land plants grow from seeds. These plants reproduce by making seeds. Seeds are made in the flower of a plant.

Plant seeds are made from **ova** (ō′və) and **pollen** (pol′ən). The ova are the egg cells. Pollen are the sperm cells.

ova
egg cells

pollen
fine powder on flowers which carries a plant's sperm cells

From one flower

In some plants, one part of the flower makes the ova. Another part of the same flower makes the pollen. When the pollen joins the ova, new cells are formed. They will become seeds that can grow into new plants.

From two flowers

In other plants, some flowers make just pollen. Other flowers make just ova. The pollen from one flower must join the ova from another flower.

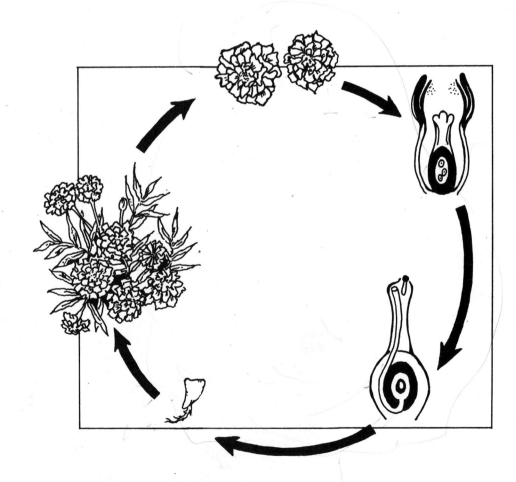

The same kind of plant

Ova won't develop into seeds that can grow unless they get pollen from the same kind of plant.

Pollen from a peach blossom and the ova from a peach blossom join and develop into a peach seed. But the pollen from a peach blossom could never make the ova in an apple blossom develop into seeds.

apple blossoms

peach blossoms

A tiny plant

When an **ovum** joins with pollen, a new cell is formed. This cell then begins to split into new cells. Each cell divides again and again until there are millions of cells. These cells become a tiny, tiny plant. It is called an **embryo** (em′ brē ō).

The embryo will some day grow into a new plant. Some cells of the embryo will be the stem. Some will be the leaves. Some will be the root.

The embryo has its own food supply around it. The embryo and its food supply are called a **seed.** The food can keep the embryo alive until the seed is planted and the tiny plant starts growing. When the new plant has leaves, it can make food for itself.

embryo
an animal or plant in its beginning stage

seed
a plant embryo with its food supply

212

When you eat beans or peas or nuts, you are eating seeds. Soak some lima beans overnight in a jar of water, then split them open. You should be able to see the embryo plants. Can you find their food?

Look at other seeds through a hand lens. Look at peanuts and corn. What can you see?

The cells divide

Animals and plants start as one cell. This cell then divides in two. Each of the two cells then divides. On and on the cells grow and divide. Soon the animal or plant has many cells. Some of the cells are different.

If cells did not divide, living things could not grow. If cells did not reproduce themselves, there would be no new living things.

What do you think living things would be like if cells could reproduce themselves, but were all alike? Would there be trees and grass and flowers? Would there be whales and sparrows and people?

SCIENCE ON THE JOB

A person who studies cells is a lab technician. You learned about cells in this unit. One thing you know is that cells are very tiny. Because of this a lab technician uses a microscope. The work must be done very carefully.

Have you had a "culture" taken from your throat? If you have, a doctor or nurse rubbed a cotton swab on the inside of your throat. The swab was then sent to a lab technician. A report was sent back to the doctor. This helped the doctor find the right medicine for you.

Other lab technicians test food samples. They can tell if food is safe to eat. If there are dangerous cells in the food, it cannot be sold.

Lab technicians work to keep us healthy.

REVIEW QUESTIONS

1. What are living things made of?
2. What are three things that all living cells do?
3. Name three important parts of cells.
4. What do plant cells have that animal cells do not?
5. What is a trait? Give some examples.
6. Name two living things that are made of just one cell.
7. What is an embryo?
8. What is a seed?

WORDS TO REVIEW

alga	cytoplasm	nucleus
amoeba	egg cell	ovum
budding	embryo	pollen
cell	heredity	seed
cell membrane	inherit	sperm cell
cell wall	nuclear membrane	trait
chloroplast		

EXPLORING FURTHER

1. Go hunting for eggs. Look for frog eggs in a pond. Look for spider webs. Can you find an egg case there? Look for egg cases on the beach.

2. Find some things in your home that act something like a cell membrane. How are they like a cell membrane?

3. You can learn how to use a microscope. Look in the newspaper for words with tiny letters. Cut out a letter "e" and put it in a drop of water on a glass slide. Look at the "e" through the microscope. What do you see? Now push the slide slightly to the left while you are looking at the "e" through the microscope. In which direction did the letter move?

4. What would happen if you cut away most of the food supply before you planted some embryo lima beans? Try it and find out.

5. Here are some books you may want to read.

   HOW PLANTS ARE MADE by Martin J. Gutnik

   THE FIRST BOOK OF MICROBES by Lucia Lewis

   AMOEBA by Sean Morrison

   HOW PLANTS ARE POLLINATED by Joan Elma Rahn

   THE HIDDEN MAGIC OF SEEDS by Dorothy E. Shuttlesworth

Unit 8
Heat Energy

Does an ice cube have heat in it?

Can heat make things move?

Where does heat come from?

219

What is heat?

Think of things that give off heat. Do you think of the summer sun? Do you think of wood burning in a fireplace or a campfire? Do you think of a bowl of hot soup?

Heat flows from hotter things to colder things. The heat from the hot campfire helps to keep our bodies warm. The heat from the bowl of hot soup makes the table warm where it sits. Heat from the sun melts the snow on a mild winter day.

How much heat?

When a hot thing gives off heat, it gets colder. Its temperature goes down. When a cold thing takes in heat, it gets warmer. Its temperature goes up. Temperature is one way to tell if heat is flowing into or out of something.

If you heat water on a stove, its temperature rises. Heat flows from the hot stove to the colder water. But the water can only get so hot. When the water reaches 100°C (212°F) it starts to boil. Now heat from the stove changes the water to a gas called steam.

When you put a tray of water into a freezer, it gets colder. Heat flows from the water to the colder freezer. But the water can only get so cold. When the temperature reaches 0°C (32°F) it freezes. So the flow of heat makes things change. Either the temperature changes, or the thing itself changes.

One kind of energy

If someone says that you have a lot of **energy,** that means that you can work hard and play hard. Heat is a kind of energy. We can make heat from other kinds of energy. Wood and gas are **fuels.** Fuels have stored energy. A turning wheel has energy. The sun has energy.

energy
stored-up work

fuel
anything that burns and gives heat energy

Different kinds of energy

There is energy stored in everything. This energy can be changed into heat. When wood burns, stored energy is changed to heat. This kind of stored energy is called **chemical** (kem'ə kl) **energy.** Oil, gas, and coal have chemical energy. You have chemical energy stored in your body.

chemical energy
stored energy that is given off when something burns

Motion makes things hot. Rub your hands together. Rub them hard and fast. How do your hands feel? Your energy was changed to heat. This kind of energy is called **mechanical** (mə kan'ə kl) **energy.**

mechanical energy
energy of movement

Electricity can be changed to heat. This happens when electricity moves through special wires. Heat made this way uses **electrical** (i lek'trə kl) **energy.** Hot plates, toasters, and some stoves make heat this way.

electrical energy
kind of energy that flows through wires

Where does energy come from?

You have learned that heat is one kind of energy. There is also chemical, mechanical, electrical, and light energy. All of these can be changed to heat energy.

When a piece of wood or coal burns, heat is produced. What is left after the wood is burned? Could this stuff be put back to form wood again? More wood can come from other trees. But how was that wood made?

You know that trees are plants. As plants, they need air, water, and sunlight. The air and water are here on earth. The sunlight gives energy to the trees. The trees use the energy to make new cells. They store some of the energy. If wood is burned, it gives back the energy. The energy comes back as heat. Is there another kind of energy given back? Think of a fireplace or campfire again.

Usually when we want to do work we don't think of getting energy from wood. We might think of a car to move people. We might think of a truck to move heavy things. Where do cars and trucks get energy? If you have ever seen a car being "filled up" at a service station, you know.

Energy from oil

Energy made from gasoline or fuel oil can be traced back to the sun.

Long ago, much of the earth was covered by seas. Small plants and animals lived in the sea. These living things died. They sank to the bottom of the sea. After many years, the layers of dead things were covered by mud. Sometimes the earth's crust changed. The sea floor was pushed up. The water flowed off. The sea floor became dry land. Still more millions of years passed. The dead plants and animals changed. They changed to oil.

Now people pump the oil from the earth. They **refine** the oil to make fuels. So when we use oil fuels, we are using stored energy. This energy came from dead plants and animals. Where did the plants and animals get the energy? We come right back to the sun again.

A lot of oil and coal are burned to make electrical energy. So when you turn on a light, you are using up more stored sun energy.

Most energy we use came to us from the sun. The energy was stored in oil and coal. It took millions of years to store. How long does it take for the sun to store energy in a tree? But we are using up the energy quickly. Why must we use this stored energy wisely?

refine
to separate and purify oil to make fuels

Sunlight makes things hotter. Put some things in bright sunlight. Feel them a little while later. How do they feel? Energy from the sun has been changed into heat.

Turn on a bright light bulb. Hold your hand near the bulb. What do you feel? What has been turned into heat? Can you trace the heat back to the sun? Make a chart to show where the heat came from.

Heat makes things change

When you think of water, you probably think of a liquid. But water can be a solid or a gas. Ice and steam are water, too.

Ice, liquid water, and steam are different forms of water. They are different **phases** (fāz). When water changes from one phase to another, heat is given off or taken in. When ice melts, it takes in heat. When water freezes, it loses heat.

phase
form of a substance

CHANGE OF PHASE

Put some ice cubes in an empty can. Put the can on a hot plate. Set the dial on the hot plate to ''low.'' Then stir the ice cubes.

When the ice begins to melt, put a thermometer into the water. What do you think is happening to the heat? Is it going into the water? Or is it going into the ice cubes? Watch the thermometer. Does the temperature of the water change? Is the heat making the water hotter? What is the heat being used for?

Adding heat

If you add heat to a solid, it will melt into a liquid. Add more heat and it will evaporate into a gas.

If you add enough heat to ice, the ice changes phase to water. If you add more heat, the water changes phase to steam.

If you add enough heat to solid steel, the steel becomes liquid. You can melt gold and silver, too. Enough heat makes these things happen.

Liquid steel pours from huge furnace

How heat moves

Heat doesn't stay in one place. Heat moves. Heat from the sun moves out through space. The sun's heat travels to earth and the other planets.

Heat moves through air and other gases. Heat moves through water and other liquids. Heat moves through earth and other solids.

Wherever it moves, heat always moves in the same direction. It moves from a hotter object, or a hotter place, to a cooler one. Heat moves from places of high temperature to places of low temperature. Heat keeps moving as long as one object, or one place, has a higher temperature than another.

From hot to cold

If you put a dish of hot food into the refrigerator, the food gets cold. Heat moves out of hot food into the cold refrigerator.

If you put a dish of ice cream on the table, the ice cream melts. Heat moves out of the warm air into the cold ice cream.

Feel a chair after someone has been sitting on it. How does it feel? Which was warmer to begin with, the person or the chair?

Heat travels through solids

You know that heat moves through metals. People use pot holders and hot pads to pick up hot cooking pans. Heat travels through metal pots and pans. People use things like pot holders to protect their hands and table tops.

The things that heat travels through easily are called **conductors** (kən duk′tər). Most metals are good conductors. Other things do not allow heat to travel well. These are called **insulators** (in′sə lā′tər). Pot holders, hot pads, and wooden handles are insulators.

conductor
substance that heat travels through easily

insulator
substance that heat does not travel through easily

TRACING THE PATH OF HEAT

You will need a candle, a paper clip, and three tiny pieces of clay. Make part of the paper clip straight by unbending it. Leave a small part bent for a handle. Place a piece of clay about 2 cm from the end of the clip. Put another piece 2 cm farther away. Put one more piece another 2 cm away. Your clip should look like this.

228

Now your teacher will light the candle. You must use care when working with candles. Do not let your clothes come near the flame.

Hold just the tip of the paper clip in the flame. Hold the clip steady. After a minute or two something will happen to the clay pieces.

Blow out the candle. After a few moments, lightly touch the middle of the clip. Has it cooled yet? Wait some more. How long does it take for the clip to cool?

Passing heat along

Heat moved through the paper clip. The heat moved from one part of the clip to the next. When the heat got near the clay, it melted and fell off. Soon more of the clip was hot. The next piece of clay fell off. Then the next. Heat had moved along the clip. When heat moves this way, it is called **conduction.**

conduction
movement of heat through a substance

You can see what happens to air when it is heated. Put an empty balloon over the neck of a soda bottle. Is there air in the bottle? Is there air in the balloon?

Put the bottle in a pan of very hot water. What happens to the balloon? Where is the air going into the balloon coming from? What do you think?

expand
to become larger

The air from the bottle is going into the balloon. Heat makes the air spread out. The air **expands.** It takes up more space. Heat makes the air move up into the balloon. The hot air pushes against the sides of the balloon. It stretches the balloon.

What happens to air when it is cooled? Here's how you can find out.

Blow up a balloon. Tie it tightly with string. Measure around the middle of the balloon with a piece of string. Mark the measurement on the string.

Put the balloon in a freezer or refrigerator. Do you think the balloon will change its size? Will it get bigger, or smaller, or stay the same?

In an hour, measure around the middle of the balloon again. What has happened?

Bring the balloon back into the warm room. Let it stay for a while. Measure it again. What has happened? What have you found out?

How much space air takes up changes. Heat makes air take up more space. Heat makes air expand.

When it gets cold, air takes up less space. The air **contracts.** It shrinks.

contract
to become smaller

237

Air in circles

Hot air is lighter than cold air. That's why hot air rises. Cold air is heavier. Cold air sinks. This makes air move in a circle. This motion of air is called **convection** (kən vek'shən).

convection
flow of energy caused by temperature differences

Air is heated by convection. As the hot air moves up, it begins to cool. When the air gets cool, it gets heavier and sinks. Hot and cold air keep changing places. They keep moving up and down. When heat moves like this, it moves by convection.

LOOKING AT CONVECTION MOVEMENT

Liquids are heated by convection, too. You can see convection movement in water.

Pour warm water into a glass. Then put an ice cube in the water. Put a few drops of food coloring on the ice.

Can you see convection movement in the water? What happens to the colored cold water? What happens to the clear warm water? Does the water move in a circle until all the water is the same temperature?

Heat travels through space

You know two ways that heat moves. Heat moves through solids, like metal, by conduction. Heat moves through liquids and gases by convection. Heat moves in another way, too.

Most of earth's heat comes from the sun. The sun's heat must travel through space. Most of space has no matter at all. Where there is no matter there is a **vacuum.** Heat travels through space by **radiation.** We get the sun's heat and light by radiation.

vacuum
a place where there is no matter

radiation
flow of energy through space

The sun's rays

The sun's rays pass through some things. Air and clear glass let most of the sunlight pass through. But some things do not let most of the sun's rays pass through.

Think of a day when the sky is filled with clouds. Not much sun reaches you on a cloudy day. The clouds **reflect** the sun's rays. Reflect means to turn back. Clouds turn back some of the sun's rays.

reflect
to bounce or turn back

Other things reflect the sun's rays, too. Snow and shiny metal turn back sun's rays. So do light-colored buildings.

Some things take in the sun's rays. Then the sun's rays are **absorbed.** Soil absorbs much of the sunlight that hits it. Rock and sand absorb the sun's rays, too. So do the oceans. The absorbed heat in rocks, sand, soil, and oceans heat the air around earth.

absorb
to take in and hold

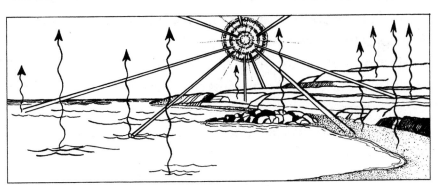

SCIENCE ON THE JOB

Automobiles and trucks depend on heat energy for power. Many people work at building autos in large factories.

In an auto engine, heat energy is changed to mechanical energy. Can you see where the word "mechanic" comes from? Mechanics repair things that break down. They know how to fix engines and other parts of autos and trucks.

Other workers also help. Gasoline station attendants put in fuel and check oil and tires. Body shop workers repair dents or rust spots.

Autos that are kept in good repair are safer and don't cause pollution. They use less energy, too.

Auto workers help provide something very important to a busy country.

REVIEW QUESTIONS

1. Name four kinds of energy.
2. What does a thermometer measure?
3. What is given off or taken in when water changes from one phase to another?
4. How does heat move? Name three ways.
5. What is temperature?
6. What is heat?

WORDS TO REVIEW

absorb	electrical energy	mechanical energy
chemical energy	energy	phase
conductor	expand	radiation
contract	fuel	refine
convection	heat	reflect
	insulator	vacuum

EXPLORING FURTHER

1. How is your school building heated? Where is the source of heat? How does the heat get into your classroom? Write a report about what you find.

2. Put a metal spoon into a glass of hot water. Hold the handle of the spoon. What happens? How did heat get into the spoon handle?

3. Open the windows, top and bottom. Find out how the air is moving. Where is the cold air? Is it going out or coming in? Where is the warm air? Is it going out or coming in?

    Draw a picture with arrows showing how hot or cold air moves in the room.

4. Charcoal can be used as a fuel. Find out how charcoal is made. Write a report.

5. Here are some books you may want to read.

    ENERGY by Irving Adler

    WHAT MAKES THE SUN SHINE? by Isaac Asimov

    WHY THINGS WORK: A BOOK ABOUT ENERGY by Jeanne Bendick

    ENERGY FROM THE SUN by Melvin Berger

    SUN POWER by Norman F. Smith

Appendix

The Metric System

Most measurements in science use the Metric System. Metric is the measuring system used in most of the world. The Metric system is easy to use. Length and mass are in metric units in this book. English units are shown in parentheses.

Length

The **meter** is the standard unit of length. Sometimes meter is spelled metre, or a symbol **m** is used. The meter is divided into 100 centimeters. A symbol **cm** can be used in place of the word centimeter. The edge of this paper is marked in centimeters. You can make a metric ruler by copying the marks on a cardboard strip.

When small measures are needed, a meter is divided into 1000 millimeters. The symbol **mm** can be used. A part of the ruler on this page is marked in millimeters.

For larger units, 1000 meters are used. The word kilometer, or symbol **km,** stands for 1000 meters.

Mass

An equal-arm balance can be used to measure the mass of something. (Mass and weight are the same at most places on earth.)

The metric unit for mass is the **gram.** The symbol **g** can be used. A gram is a small unit. Two paper clips equal one gram. A nickel weighs 5 grams.

To measure things with more mass, the kilogram is used. A kilogram is 1000 grams. The symbol **kg** can be used. A brick has a mass of about 1 kg. Your body has a mass of about 35 kg.

Science Words

The words listed here will help you to learn and use the language of science. To help you understand and pronounce these words, both definitions and a guide to pronunciation are provided for you.

Some science words are difficult to define in one or two sentences. Science words sometimes have more than one meaning. Fortunately, these are the exception rather than the rule. The definitions used here are ones which most closely explain and define the words as they are used in this book. The numbers after each definition tells you on what pages you can find the word used in the book.

As you are studying science throughout the year, perhaps you will want to use this section as another kind of index. The words listed are the ones most important to your year's study of science.

Pronunciation Key

The pronunciation of many words is shown just after the word, in this way: territory (ter′ə tô′rē). The letters and signs used are pronounced as in the words below. The mark ′ is placed after a syllable with primary or heavy accent, as in the example above. The mark ′ after a syllable shows a secondary or lighter accent.

a	hat, cap	i	it, pin	p	paper, cup	v	very, save
ā	age, face	ī	ice, five	r	run, try	w	will, woman
ã	care, air					y	young, yet
ä	father, far	j	jam, enjoy	s	say, yes		
		k	kind, seek	sh	she, rush	z	zero, breeze
b	bad, rob	l	land, coal			zh	measure, seizure
ch	child, much	m	me, am	t	tell, it		
d	did, red			th	thin, both		
		n	no, in	ŦH	then, smooth	ə	represents:
e	let, best	ng	long, bring				a in about
ē	equal, be			u	cup, butter		e in taken
ėr	term, learn	o	hot, rock	ù	full, put		i in April
		ō	open, go	ü	rule, move		o in lemon
f	fat, if	ô	order, all	ū	use, music		u in circus
g	go, bag	oi	oil, voice				
h	he, how	ou	house, out				

From THORNDIKE–BARNHART JUNIOR DICTIONARY by E. L. Thorndike and Clarence L. Barnhart. Copyright © 1968 by Scott, Foresman and Company. Reprinted by permission.

absorb (ab sôrb′)   to take in and hold; 241

adapt (ə dapt′)   fit to a certain way of life; 110

aircraft   object that can be floated or flown through the air; 56

air pressure   the pushing force of air; 175

air traffic controller   a person who directs airplanes as they land and take off; 59

Aleutian (ə lü′shən) **Islands**   islands near Alaska formed by volcanoes; 145

alga (al′gə)   simple living thing that does not have true stems, leaves, or roots; pl. algae (al′jē); 12, 206

amoeba (ə mē′bə)   a tiny, one-celled animal; 206

amphibian (am fib′ē ən)   an animal that lives both on land and in water. A frog is an amphibian; 25, 82

Appalachian (ap′ə lā′chən) **Mountains**   a mountain range that stretches from Canada to Alabama; 146

atmosphere (at′məs fir)   the air around earth; 127

attract (ə trakt′)   to pull close together; 171

backbone   the main bone supporting the skeleton in certain groups of animals. Mammals, birds, reptiles, amphibians, and fish all have backbones; 23

basalt (bə sôlt′)   a dark rock heavier than granite and making up earth's crust under the oceans; 134

behavior (bi hāv′yər)   the way an animal acts; 76

budding   reproducing by having a part of a living thing grow and break off, forming another similar living thing; 207

burrow (bėr′ō)   a hole dug in the ground by an animal; 118

cell (sel)   a small unit of living material. All living things are made of cells; 192

cell membrane (mem′brān)   thin lining that encloses a cell; 196

cell wall   outer, nonliving boundary of a plant cell; 200

chameleon (kə mē′lē ən)   a lizard that can change the color of its skin; 68, 74, 80

chemical (kem′ə kl) **energy**   stored energy that is given off when something burns; 223

chloroplast (klör′ə plast)   one of many tiny green parts in most green plant cells; 200

circuit (sėr′kit)   a path through which electricity flows; 183

classify (klas′ə fī)   to divide into groups; 10

cloud   visible water vapor in the sky; 38, 53

cold-blooded   able to keep body temperature at or near the same as the environment; 29

community (kə mū′nə tē)   all the living things that are part of a neighborhood; 64

conduction (kən duk′shən)   the movement of heat or electricity through a substance; 235

conductor (kən duk′tər)   a substance heat or electricity travels through easily; 233

cone   a scaly pod with seeds of an evergreen; 17

continent (kont′n ənt)   one of the big land areas of the world. North America is a continent; 134

contract (kən trakt′)   to become smaller; 237

contrail (kon′trāl)   trail of vapor left by a plane flying at high altitude; 53

convection (kən vek′shən)   the movement of heat from one place to another by the motion of liquids or gases; 238

crust (krust)   earth's outer layer of rock. The crust is about 20 miles thick unde the continents and about 3 miles thick under the oceans; 130

current electricity (i lek′tris′ə tē)   electricity flowing through a wire; 183

cytoplasm (sī′tə plaz′əm)   cell material outside the nucleus; 196

dewlap (dü′lap′)   a loose flap of skin under the throat of a chameleon; 74

dolphin (dol′fən)   a sea mammal; 117

earthquake   a sudden movement of earth's crust; 137

egg cell (eg sel)   a tiny cell produced by the female. When an egg cell and a sperm cell come together, they make a new organism; 208

electrical (i lek'trə kl) **energy**   kind of energy that flows through wires; 223

embryo (em'brē ō)   an animal or plant in its beginning stage, before birth, hatching, or sprouting; 212

energy (en'ər jē)   stored-up work; 222

expand (eks pand')   to become larger; 236

experience (eks pir'ē əns)   all the things that have ever happened to you or to another organism; 94

extinct (eks tingkt')   no longer found alive anywhere on earth; 26

fault (fôlt)   a break in earth's crust; 135

fern   plant with featherlike leaves that grow from spores; 15

fog   a low cloud; 53

force (fôrs)   a push or pull that changes the speed or direction of motion of an object; 158

friction (frik'shən)   a force that slows down objects that are moving; 179

fuel (fū'əl)   anything that burns and gives heat energy; 222

fungus (fung'gəs)   plant that can't make its own food; pl. fungi (fun'jī); 113

gill (gil)   the breathing organ of an animal that takes oxygen from the water; 24

glacier (glā'shər)   large mass of ice, formed from snow, that moves slowly downhill; 129

granite (gran'it)   a very hard rock. The continents are mostly granite; 134

gravity (grav'ə tē)   a force that pulls everything on earth toward the center of earth; 164

ground water   water below the surface of earth; 128

heredity (hə red'ə tē)   all the traits a cell or an organism gets from its parents; 204

hoof   the hard material that covers the feet of some animals; 116

horizon (hə rī'zn)   the line where earth and sky seem to meet; 40

hurricane (hér'ə kān)   a storm with heavy rains and strong winds; 139

iceberg   a mass of ice broken away from a glacier and floating in the ocean; 129

imprinting (im print'ing)   behavior learned early in life that involves recognizing and being attracted to something; 93

inherit (in her'it)   receive a trait from parents; 203

insect (in'sekt)   a small air-breathing animal without a backbone, but with a three-part body and three pairs of legs; 22, 85

instinct (in'stingkt)   unlearned behavior that an animal is born with; 92

insulator (in'sə lā'tər)   substance that heat or electricity does not travel through easily; 233

island arc   curving chain of volcanic islands; 145

koala (kō ä'lə)   a tree-dwelling animal with thick fur, sharp claws and large ears; 120

larva (lär'və)   an early stage in the development of an insect; pl. larvae; 86, 90

limb (lim)   an arm, a leg, a flipper, or a wing. People stand on two limbs; 106–107, 112

lines of force   imaginary curved lines connecting the north and south poles of magnets; 172

lung (lung)   one of a pair of breathing organs that contain air, from which the blood takes up oxygen and gives up carbon dioxide; 25, 108

magnet (mag'nit)   a piece of iron or steel that will attract other iron or steel; 168

magnetic field   the space around a magnet where its magnetic force can be detected; 172

magnetic force   the push or pull of a magnet; 168

magnetic pole   a place on a magnet where its force seems to be strongest; 168

mammal (mam′l)   an air-breathing, warm-blooded animal with a backbone and hair somewhere on its body. Female mammals make milk for their young; 30, 102

marsupial (mär sü′pē əl)   a mammal with a pouch; 120

mechanical (mə kan′ə kəl) **energy**   energy of movement; 223

meteor (mē′tē ər)   a piece of space material that burns up before reaching earth; 54

microscope (mī′krə skōp)   an instrument that makes an object appear larger; 195, 202

model (mod′l)   something we make to see how something else looks or works; 50

mold (mōld)   fuzzy plants that grow on bread or rotting fruit; 13

neighborhood (nā′bər hůd)   a place made up of both living and nonliving things; 64

northern lights   streamers or bands of light that appear over the North Pole; 55

nuclear (nü′klē ər) **membrane**   thin lining which encloses a cell nucleus; 197

nucleus (nü′klē əs)   an important part of a cell. Without a nucleus, a cell cannot reproduce or even stay alive; 196

opossum (ə pos′əm)   a small animal that lives in a tree and has a long tail; 120

orangutan (ô rang′ü tan′)   reddish-colored ape that lives on the islands of Borneo and Sumatra; 115

ovum (ō′vum)   an egg cell; pl. ova; 209

oxygen (ok′sə jən)   a gas in the air that animals breathe; 24, 108

phase (fāz)   form of a substance; 229

planet (plan′it)   an object, such as Mars, that orbits around a star, such as the sun; 44

plate   large piece of earth's crust; 135

pollen (pol′ən)   the fine powder on flowers which produces a plant's sperm cells; 209

porpoise (pôr′pəs)   a sea mammal; 117

queen ant   the only female ant to have wings and the ability to lay eggs; 89

radiation (rā′dē ā′shən)   the flow of energy through space; 240

rainbow   arch of colors across the sky; 52

react   to act in answer to some action; 9

reason   think things out; 94

refine   separate and purify oil to make fuels; 227

reflect ri flekt′)   to turn or bounce back; 41, 241

repel (ri pel′)   to push away; 171

reproduce (rē′prə düs′)   to produce the same kind of living thing; 9, 103

reptile (rep′tl)   a cold-blooded animal, usually covered with scales, with a backbone and lungs; 26, 28, 80

response (ri spons′)   the reaction of a living thing to a stimulus; 77

rhinoceros (rī nos′ər əs)   a mammal with hooves; 116

rodent (rōd′nt)   a small mammal that uses its teeth for gnawing; 113

salamander (sal′ə man′dər)   an amphibian that lives in dark, woodsy places; 72, 84

San Andreas Fault   a crack in earth's surface in California; 135, 137

seed   a plant embryo and its food supply; 209, 212

skeleton (skel′ə tən)   all the bones of an animal's body, fitted together to give the body support; 105

spacecraft   thing used for travel outside earth's air layer; 56

spectrum (spek′trəm) the band of colors produced when light is broken up; 52

sperm cell (sperm sel) a tiny cell produced by the male. When a sperm cell and an egg come together, they make a new organism; 208

sphere (sfir) a round object; 133

sponge (spunj) simple animal that usually lives in salt water; 20

spore (spôr) reproductive part of fungi and ferns; 13, 15

star a very large object that radiates its own energy, such as the sun; 38, 44

static electricity (i lek′tris′ə tē) electric charges that are not in motion; 182

stimulus (stim′yə ləs) a change inside or around a living thing that makes it respond; 77

terrarium (tə rãr′ē əm) a glass container holding growing plants and living animals; 66

territory (ter′ə tô′rē) an animal's living space; 70

trait (trāt) a characteristic inherited from parents; 203

trench a long, narrow depression on the ocean floor; 151

tyrannosaurus (tə ran′ə sôr′əs) a very strong dinosaur, or reptile, now extinct; 26

UFO an unknown object in the sky; 58

vacuum (vāk′yù əm) a place where there is no matter; 240

valley land that lies between ranges of mountains or hills; 150

vector (vek′tər) an arrow that shows the amount and direction of a force; 163

veterinarian (vet′ər ə nãr′ē ən) a doctor who treats animals; 121

volcano (vol kā′nō) a mountain built by outpourings of liquid rock, fine dust, and pieces of solid rock; 137

warm-blooded able to keep body temperature at or very near a certain level regardless of surrounding temperatures; 29, 109

weight (wāt) the amount of gravity pulling on an object; 167

worker ant one of the most numerous kind of ant in an ant community; 88

Index

absorb, 241
adapt, 110–113, 117–118,
air, 38, 40, 42, 52,
    126–127, 164, 241
    and living things, 9,
        11, 108, 224
    cooled, 53, 237–238
    force of, 175
    friction of, 180
    heat in, 220, 232,
        236–238
    movement of, 238
    pressure, 175–178
    temperature, 57
air traffic controllers, 59
aircraft, 56
airplanes, 50, 53, 56, 58,
    176–177
Aleutian Islands, 145
algae, 12, 19, 206
amoeba, 206
amphibians, 25, 29, 82–84
animals, 12, 19, 32, 65,
    192, 203
    classifying, 10–11,
        19–32
    cold-blooded, 29
    hoofed, 116
    move, 11, 22,
        106–107, 122–114
    soil, 74–75
    terrarium, 66–84
    warm-blooded, 29–30,
        109, 120
    with backbones,
        23–30
    with bumpy skin, 21
    with jointed legs, 22
    with sac bodies, 20
    with soft bodies, 21
antennae, 89
ants, 85–92, 95, 111, 192
    eggs, 86, 88–90

home for, 86–87
larvae, 86, 88, 90
queen, 86, 89–90
soldier, 88
worker, 88, 89, 91
apes, 114–115
Appalachian Mountains,
    146
atmosphere, 127
attract, 170–171
auto workers, 242

backbones, 23–30, 106
basalt, 134
bats, 113
behavior, 76–95
birds, 29, 32, 93
blood, 109, 195
bones, 23, 29, 81, 105,
    112–113, 193
budding, 207
burrow, 118

caterpillar, 92
cell membrane, 196–200
cell wall, 200, 207
cells, 192–215
    animal, 195
    are alike, 194–195,
        200, 202
    divide, 208, 212, 214
    egg, 205, 208–209
    kinds of, 193
    onion, 195, 202
    parts of, 196–197,
        200
    plant, 195, 200–202
    size and shape of,
        192, 200
    sperm, 208–209
chameleon, 68, 74–75,
    79–80
chloroplasts, 200, 202

circuit, 183–185
classifying, 10–11, 16,
    31–32
clouds, 38, 52–53, 128,
    241
cocoon, 92
comet, 44
community, 64–95
    ant, 88
    desert, 65
    forest, 65
    jungle, 65
    making a, 66
    pond, 65
compass, 171
conduction, 235, 240
conductors, 233
cones, 17
continents, 134
contract, 237
contrails, 53
convection, 238–240
crust, 130–131, 134–139,
    146, 152
current electricity,
    183–185
cytoplasm, 196–197

Death Valley, 150
dewlap, 74, 79
dinosaurs, 24, 26–27
direction, 164, 171
    change of, 159–160

earth, 45, 50, 126–152,
    232
    changes, 139–147,
        153, 226
    crust, 130–131,
        134–139, 146, 152,
        226
    force of, 164–167

magnetic poles, 168, 171
model of, 51
motion of, 40, 48, 49
parts of, 126–131
shape of, 47, 49, 51, 132–133
earthquakes, 133, 137–139, 152
egg, 28, 32, 103
    ant, 86, 88–90
    bird, 93, 103
    cell, 205, 208–209
    chicken, 192
    fish, 103
    mammal, 120
egg cell, 205, 208–209
electricity, 182, 223
    current, 182–185
    static, 182
embryo, 212–213
energy, 222–228
    cells and, 194, 224
    chemical, 223–224
    electrical, 223–224, 227
    from oil, 226–227
    from sun, 222, 226, 228
    heat, 220–241
    light, 224
    mechanical, 223–224
    solar, 228
expand, 141, 236–237
experience, 94–95
extinct, 26

fault, 135
    San Andreas, 135, 137
ferns, 15, 67
fish, 24, 25, 29, 108
flowers, 11, 16, 209–211

flying saucers, 58
fog, 53
force, 158–185
    direction of, 163
    earth's, 164–167
    electrical, 182–186
    friction, 179
    lines of, 172–173
    magnetic, 168–173, 186
    muscle, 166
    of air and wind, 175
    water, 166
friction, 179–182
frogs, 25, 68, 71–73, 75, 79, 82, 84–85, 103
    cells of, 192, 195
    tree, 73
fruits, 16–17
fuels, 222, 226–227
fungi, 13

game wardens, 33
gases, 126–127, 229, 232, 240
gills, 24–25, 108
glaciers, 129, 141, 144
globe, 51, 134
Grand Canyon, 140
granite, 134
grasses, 17
gravity, 164–167, 176–177
ground water, 128

heart, 109
heat, 79, 181, 220–241
    movement of, 232–241
heredity, 204
hoof, 116
horizon, 40–42
hurricane, 139

icebergs, 129
imprinting, 93, 95
in-betweens, 25
    in water, 12
    on land, 13
inherit, 203–204
insects, 22, 80–82, 84, 118
    social, 85
instinct, 92, 94–95
insulators, 233
island arcs, 145
islands, 139, 145
    Aleutian, 145

koala, 120

lab technician, 215
larvae, ant, 86, 88, 90
learn, 30, 93–95
leaves, 11, 15
    cells of, 201, 212
light,
    bending of, 52
    from the sun, 38–41, 52
    reflected, 41, 56–57
    scattered, 38–39, 42
lightning, 54, 182
limbs, 106–107, 112–113, 115, 120
lines of force, 172–173
liquids, 126, 128, 136, 229, 231–232, 239–240
lizards, 26, 65
lungs, 25, 28, 108, 127

machines, 181
magnetic fields, 172
magnetic force, 168–173, 186
magnetic poles, 168–169, 172

magnets, 168–173
mammals, 30, 32, 102–120
    bones of, 105, 120
    egg-laying, 120
    growth of, 103, 120
    hair of, 104, 110, 120
    insect-eating, 118
    looking for, 119
    meat-eating, 118
    milk of, 103, 120
    pouched, 120
    young of, 103, 120
membrane,
    cell, 196–202
    nuclear, 197
meteors, 54
microscope, 12, 20, 192, 195, 197, 200, 202, 215
models, 50–51
    cell membrane, 198–199
    earth, 51
molds, 13, 15
monkeys, 65, 114–115, 192
moon, 41–46, 48, 52, 54
moss, 15, 66, 84
mountains, 139, 140–141, 144–151
    Appalachian, 146
Mt. Everest, 148, 151
Mt. McKinley, 149
Mt. Mitchell, 149
muscles, 105, 112
    cells of, 193
mushrooms, 13, 15
    printing with, 14

neighborhood, 64
North Pole, 55
northern lights, 55
nuclear membrane, 197

nucleus, 196–197
    membrane of, 197

ocean, 126, 128–129, 131–132, 134–135, 140, 151–152, 221, 241
oil, 181, 223
    energy from 226–227
opossum, 120
onion cells, 195, 202
ovum, 209–212
oxygen, 24, 108, 127
    cells need of, 194, 197

parents, 203–204, 206, 208
phases, 229–231
planets, 44, 54, 232
plants, 11–12, 19, 32, 65, 192, 203, 210–212, 224
    cells of, 209–212
    classifying, 10–19
    flowering, 16
    seeds of, 209–213
    with seeds, 16–18
    without seeds, 15
plates, 135–138, 146, 151–152
pole,
    magnetic, 168–172
    North, 55
pollen, 209–212
ponds, 20, 65, 67–68, 72, 75, 80, 128
    algae in, 12
pressure, 146

radiation, 240
rainbow, 36–37, 52
react, 9, 11
reason, 94–95
records, 42–43, 48, 50, 52, 76, 80, 153

refine, 227
reflect, 41, 56–57, 241
repel, 170–171
reproduce, 9, 15, 28, 103, 194, 197, 206–209, 214
reptiles, 26–28, 29, 80–81
response, 77–80
rock, 130–131, 140–141, 241
    liquid, 136
rockets, 56, 165
rodents, 113
roots, 11, 201
    cells of, 201, 212

salamanders, 68, 72, 75, 84
San Andreas Fault, 135, 137
sand dunes, 142
satellites, 56, 58
scales, 80
seeds, 11, 205, 209–213
    one-part, 16–17
    plants with, 16–18
    plants without, 15
    two-part, 16
shells, 20–21, 28, 81
    of algae, 12
skeletons, 20, 22, 105
sky, 38–58
snakes, 26, 103
soil, 126, 130, 140, 142, 241
solids, 126, 229, 231–233, 240
spacecraft, 56, 165
spaceships, 58
spectrum, 52
speed, change of, 161–162, 179
sperm cell, 208–209
sphere, 133

sponges, 20
spores, 13–15
stars, 38, 44–45, 48, 54
static electricity, 182
stems, 11, 201
    cells of, 201, 212
stimulus, 77–80, 89
sun, 38–41, 45–46, 48, 50
    energy from, 222,
        226, 228, 232,
        240–241
sunlight, 40–42, 44, 56,
    67, 224, 228, 241
sunrise, 42
sunset, 40, 42
surveyors, 153

teachers, 96
teeth, 32, 111, 113, 118
telephone workers, 186
temperature, 221–222,
    230, 232, 239
    of air, 57
    of the body, 79, 109

terrarium, 66–84
    building a, 67–68
territory, 70–71, 75
thermometers, 221, 230
toads, 71, 75, 83–84
traits, 203–204
tree frogs, 73
trees, 17, 192, 224
    cones of, 17
    learning about, 18
trenches, 151
turtles, 26, 68, 72, 75, 79,
    81, 85

UFO, 58

vacuum, 240
valleys, 141, 150–151
vectors, 163, 175
veterinarian, 121
volcanoes, 137, 139,
    144–145, 152

water,
    and living things, 11,
        201, 224
    as part of earth,
        128–129, 131
    changes earth,
        140–141, 144
    force of, 166, 178
    heat in, 220, 232
    in-betweens in, 12
    in the air, 38, 40,
        52–53
    in the ground, 128
    phases of, 229–231
weather, 139
weather balloons, 57–58
weight, 167, 175
whales, 117
wind,
    changes earth,
        142–144
    force of, 175
    speed, 57
wings, 29
    airplane, 176–177

yeast, budding, 207

BCDEFGH08543210
Printed in the United States of America